T0012992

'This raw, honest account of semi[...] lesson in how to find beauty and w[...] cumstances ... Campbell is wonderfully alert to every [...] experience, and writes with joyous precision about the summer she sees unfolding all around her.'
The Scotsman

'A "many-splendoured" book, which is at once an after-love, ever-loving letter to her ex; a real-time journal to keep herself company and emotionally intact; a worked-over piece of literary art (Campbell writes beautiful prose) and a rich newcomer to the latest and most exciting department of place writing.'
Horatio Clare, *Spectator*

'A courageous, compassionate, uncanny chronicle of life and loss on the fringes. Striking in its candour, brilliant in its breadth, often very funny.'
Dan Richards, author of *Outpost*

'A memoir of great honesty and clarity, intimacy and subtlety ... It asks profound questions about how to live through the storms of life with authenticity.'
Gavin Francis, author of *Adventures in Human Being*

'Rich and moving ... deeply cathartic ... tender and warm ... A deep exploration of mental health, mortality, and our connection with place.'
Kate Blincoe, *Resurgence & Ecologist*

'One is swept along by the subtle, elegant prose and a narrative that is rich in literary references, sometimes carried away by poetic drift, yet overridingly a visceral, energising sense of a life live well.'
Country Life

'Hopeful, honest and lyrically written, a memoir which celebrates resilience in precarious times.'
The Simple Things

'Any book by Nancy Campbell has to be worth reading.'
Dervla Murphy

'A humbling, honest, raw and deeply moving book that reminds us what it means to be alive. What it means to be human, to be ill, to be in communion with all with which we share this earth . . . how we dance through the songs we are given – no matter how dark or troubling the lines may be.'
Kerri ní Dochartaigh, author of *Thin Places*

'Such a compelling account of deliberate living, in the best tradition of Thoreau, Dillard and Roger Deakin. Nancy Campbell's deep knowledge of art, nature and other cultures is completely transporting, even while her story is set over a single year in a small caravan marooned in middle England. She blends the intensely local with the wider world with such skill. I couldn't put it down.'
Tanya Shadrick, author of *The Cure For Sleep*

'One has the rare sense, reading this book, of a work that emerged fully formed. Vivid, intense, wry and clarified, as Campbell steps fully into the frame, she simultaneously makes a case for empty spaces: for the gaps, absences and edgelands through which change first comes . . . If this is a story of grief and illness, loneliness and heartache, one is left with the feeling that here is a writer who knows better than most of us how to *live*.'
Helen Jukes, author of *A Honeybee Heart Has Five Openings*

'Nancy Campbell renders her life through the eyes of a poet from the midst of hardship, in scenes that are by turns humbling, humorous and exquisite. Her words dazzle like mica in the flow of a muddy river.'
Sarah Thomas, author of *The Raven's Nest*

'Peppering her poetic prose with fascinating stories and close observations of the natural world, Nancy Campbell brings us into the woods with her as she wrestles with the practicalities and emotional fallout of living alone in a remote caravan. As Campbell rebuilds her life she explores deeper issues of belonging, friendship and how to live with courage.'
Lulah Ellender, author of *Grounding*

'*Thunderstone* goes well beyond mere memoir. Nancy is a badass, a wild woman corralling experiences of poetry, humanity and the natural world to shape visions of new ways forward for us all. Her forgotten nettle-patch beyond the boundaries of civilisation becomes a resonant setting for what is a work of the richest travel literature, written from a place of deliberate isolation. You carry it with you, long after finishing.'
Matthew Teller, author of *Nine Quarters of Jerusalem*

'The *terra nova* Nancy Campbell discovers in *Thunderstone* lies close to home – a pocket of overlooked and semi-derelict land alongside a railway line and canal in Oxford . . . This isn't the city she has known, on and off, for two decades; but from the vantage point of her new home, she can see it, and the world that stretches beyond, through a fresh lens.'
James Attlee, author of *Under the Rainbow: Voices from Lockdown*

'Nancy Campbell writes of a world that has been shattered and reassembled, weaving intricate new patterns from the debris of the old. A writer of quiet strength, clarity and empathy, with a traveller's eye for detail and the precision of a poet, she is the wisest and kindest of guides through heartbreak and beyond.'
Nick Hunt, author of *Outlandish*

thunderstone

FINDING SHELTER FROM THE STORM

NANCY CAMPBELL

Elliott&Thompson

First published 2022 by
Elliott and Thompson Limited
2 John Street
London WC1N 2ES
www.eandtbooks.com

This paperback edition published in 2023

ISBN: 978-1-78396-699-8

Permissions:
p. 1 and p. 187: 'On Being Ill' in *The Moment and Other Essays* by Virginia Woolf, used courtesy of The Society of Authors as the Literary Representative of the Estate of Virginia Woolf; pp. 31, 72, 87, 125: E. M. Forster's *Howards End*, used courtesy of The Provost and Scholars of King's College, Cambridge and the Society of Authors as the E. M. Forster Estate; p. 38: *Into Their Labours* © John Berger, and John Berger Estate, 1979; p. 96: Excerpt from NOX copyright © 2010 by Anne Carson. Reprinted by permission of New Directions Publishing Corp; p. 107: 'Oxford revisited' in *The Golden Hynde: And Other Poems* by Alfred Noyes, used courtesy of The Society of Authors as the Literary Representative of the Estate of Alfred Noyes; p. 114: Reproduced from GOODBYE TO ALL THAT by Robert Graves (Copyright © Robert Graves Trust 1929) by permission of United Agents LLP (www.unitedagents.co.uk) on behalf of Accuro Trustees (Jersey) Ltd as trustees of the Robert Graves Copyright Trust; p. 122: *This Little Art*, Kate Briggs, copyright © Kate Briggs, 2017. Reproduced by permission of Fitzcarraldo Editions; p. 147: 'Days' from *So Much for That Winter: Novellas* by Dorthe Nors, translated from the Danish by Misha Hoekstra. Copyright © 2010 by Dorthe Nors and Rosinante & Co. Translation copyright © 2016 by Misha Hoekstra. Reprinted with the permission of The Permissions Company, LLC on behalf of Graywolf Press, www.graywolfpress.org, and with thanks to Ahlander Agency and Misha Hoekstra; p. 151: Jan Morris, *Trieste and the Meaning of Nowhere* (London, 2002), used with permission of Faber & Faber Ltd; p. 164: 'Letters from Tove' © Tove Jansson Estate, 2014; p. 165: 'Notes from an Island' © Tove Jansson 1996, Moomin Characters™; p. 169: foreword to *Faithful Witnesses* © John Berger, and John Berger Estate, 1990; p. 218: 'what would I miss', from *Sobbing Superpower: Selected Poems of Tadeusz Różewicz* by Tadeusz Różewicz, translated by Joanna Trzeciak. Copyright © 2011 by Joanna Trzeciak. Used by permission of W. W. Norton & Company, Inc.

Page 227, picture of caravan, and page 244 author photo © Nancy Campbell

9 8 7 6 5 4 3 2 1

A catalogue record for this book is available from the British Library.

Typesetting: Marie Doherty
Printed by CPI Group (UK) Ltd, Croydon, CR0 4YY

MIX
Paper | Supporting
responsible forestry
FSC® C171272

for Sarah Bodman
comrade and collaborator

all these and most other kinds of stony bodies which are
formed thus strangely figured, do owe their formation and
figuration, not to any kind of *Plastick virtue* inherent in the
earth, but to the shells of certain Shell-fishes, which, either
by some Deluge, Inundation, Earthquake, or some such
other means, came to be thrown to that place, and there
to be fill'd with some kind of Mudd or Clay, or *petrifying*
Water, or some other substance, which in tract of time
has been settled together and hardned in those shelly
mounds into those shaped substances we now find them.

ROBERT HOOKE
MICROGRAPHIA; OR, SOME PHYSIOLOGICAL
DESCRIPTIONS OF MINUTE BODIES
MADE BY MAGNIFYING GLASSES, WITH
OBSERVATIONS AND INQUIRIES THEREUPON

CONTENTS

LOCKDOWN

All day, all night the body intervenes; blunts or sharpens,
colours or discolours, turns to wax in the warmth of
June, hardens to tallow in the murk of February.
VIRGINIA WOOLF, 'ON BEING ILL'

What is your name? says the nurse.

Anna, says Anna.

Can you tell me who this is? The nurse points at me. I sit on the plastic hospital chair, my chin sunk into the collar of my coat, haggard after travelling overnight from Munich.

Nancy. Anna pronounces the two syllables carefully. There's warmth in her voice. No rising intonation, no question. I don't believe I've ever had a stronger sense of what it is to be loved than at this moment. But love isn't what I want now.

Where are you, Anna? says the nurse.

In the pub, says Anna.

As the first rumours of a virus in Wuhan circled the world, I was sitting on the fifth floor of an Oxford hospital, watching my partner as she slept. Anna's face was wan, her arms mottled by deep bruises. A baroque arrangement of tubes surrounded the bed, like briars in the fairy tale. Anna's life had been saved by a rare procedure known as mechanical thrombectomy, which sends a catheter through the blood vessels to siphon clots from the brain. I imagined the surgeon's intricate manoeuvres. As in the movies when the actor finds the combination to a safe in a race against the clock, turning a dial by torchlight in a dark room.

When Anna awoke *monster* was one of the few words she could say. *Monster!* with a look of incomprehension and terror at her own act of speech. What dark forest was she lost in? Did she mean herself or me – or something else? As the days passed she found other words, and strung them together for me to unravel: *In the pub. You have a beautiful theme.*

3

Nurses came with tests: first, a piece of paper on which was a pattern of stars. Anna was instructed to draw circles around each of them. Since her right arm was paralysed, she took the pen in her left hand, and scribbled out all the stars. 'Let's try again,' said the nurse kindly, as if it didn't really matter, presenting Anna with an identical sheet, and explaining the task once more. Anna struck through the stars furiously, as if wishing to obliterate a whole galaxy. When I left the ward, the nurse followed me. Beside the machine where you put in a coin and got a cup of bad coffee, she gave me a leaflet called *What is Communication?*

She said: 'You do know, that Anna has very severe aphasia?'

I did know. I didn't.

I put a coin in the machine, and hesitated.

'The coffee's shit,' said a voice behind me. 'My dad likes the hot chocolate.'

I punched the button for hot chocolate.

Boiling water spluttered onto the milk powder. I turned to see a man in his sixties, dressed in water-sports shorts and a T-shirt that said *Oxford Kayak Tours*. He exuded the confidence of a consultant.

'Thanks for the advice. It looks disgusting.'

He shrugged. 'You could bring her a Thermos.'

I gazed across a row of beds covered in identical blue blankets. A window ran the length of the ward, and I watched weather moving across the valley, sheets of rain muting the autumn colours of the distant woods. Oxford's dreaming spires are spoken of more often than the soft hills that hem them in. When I first arrived in the city as a student, a college doctor warned me that my lungs would miss the air of the northern moors: the Vale of the White Horse contains pollution like smoke in a bowl. The doctor could have applied his theory to people, too. I didn't intend to stay once my studies ended, but however many times I left, circumstances would draw me back. The long chalk range of the Chilterns, to the south and east, and the low scarp slope of the Berkshire Downs were gently but persuasively encircling. Through twenty years of travels, Oxford remained my *poste restante*.

Anna had allowed me the freedom to travel, but recently she had seemed to care less whether I returned. We were slipping out of each other's orbit with an ominously steady trajectory. I worked away from home more and more, and when I was offered a fellowship in Germany, I took it. Anna did not come.

A few months later, I was hosting a dinner for a wild cohort of artists in my apartment in the Künstlerhaus, a converted baroque palace beside the River Regnitz. I heard myself talking wistfully about my partner, who being an interpreter was so much better at languages than I was, then making excuses for her absence that did not even convince me as I uttered them. Later, while rinsing the delicate wine glasses, I resolved to travel back to England to have a conversation about The Future, which might mean Separating.

The night before I was due to leave, I received the phone call. The one that comes from an unknown number and rings and rings until you know you have to answer. My suitcase was already packed.

In our basement flat, I begin to unravel the disarray that amassed before Anna's hospitalisation. The briars had grown until they hid the whole castle. Scans of Anna's brain have revealed that she's suffered at least one 'undocumented' stroke in the last few years. Such a neutral word. Behind it lies an incomprehensible enormity: that Anna experienced brain trauma and did not receive help, that we continued to struggle through the days oblivious to her needs. I flick back through the calendar in my mind, again and again, wondering which moment things changed. I view our lives together in a different light. The behaviour that puzzled and disturbed me: why every time I left for a few days the flat descended into chaos, so that I dreaded returning home; the dishes unwashed, the loose change scattered over the floor, the unopened mail stuffed down the back of the bed and the sofa, inside books; one hundred small tasks begun and never completed; the spice rack that never made it onto the kitchen wall; the escalating library fines; all the mysterious tote bags lying around, each filled with lunches that were never eaten, a banana and a Müller yoghurt and a bottle of fizzy drink – some several months old, a black coagulation of the organic and the almost imperishable. In among the ordure, I find pockets of sanity even more heartbreaking than the mess: notebooks, in which Anna had written out her favourite poems since she was a teenager; her violin case; a box full of beautiful hand-painted wooden cups, the inside lacquered gold, wrapped in a Moscow newspaper from 2002.

As I stand among the junk, the realisation comes to me that Anna has been ill for a very long time. Perhaps as long as I've known her. I trace quirks of character back, wondering at their significance. An impatience of background music. That listlessness and torpor, which botched a final stab at romance this summer. I'd booked a boutique hotel in Paris, but Anna didn't want to get up to catch the Eurostar, so I went alone, to a muted enjoyment of the king-sized bed, the luxuriant claw-footed bath. My annoyance dissolves in horror that I did not see how ill my partner was. Could I have prevented her stroke with better care? I was scrupulous on my travels, precise in my observations of other places, but where had my attention been when I was at home?

During the shortest days of the year, I rattle between the damp Oxford flat and my rooms in the Künstlerhaus, aware that one represents a possible future, and one does not – but which? I put my money and my hopes on the Künstlerhaus, as I must in order to keep moving, although both seem equally dreamlike. The rose garden by the Regnitz a glistening daydream, and hospital vigils a dimly remembered nightmare. No one can choose what dreams they dream, or when they wake from them. I can board a train, but I cannot leave these visions behind.

The howl is an animal that stalks me now. A silent, unpredictable, chest-wrenching, bent-double, dribbling-out-of-a-mouth-that-will-not-close sorrow. Like all illegal and dangerous, unconventional and unsightly pets, like the packs of suburban pythons or tower-block tigers, it needs to be kept hidden away. But my howl won't stay locked in the basement we once shared. The smallest whiff of nostalgia lures it out. I'm in the ward at lunchtime when the aide brings Anna egg mayonnaise sandwiches, cut into tiny crustless triangles for patients who are in danger of choking on their food. I remember the picnics I made our first summer together. In her honour, I elevated egg mayonnaise to a high art. No dill, no mustard now. No cracked black pepper. No thinly sliced radishes. Anna makes a face, and sends the plate away.

Later that afternoon, waiting in a November rainstorm for the number 10 bus (always infrequent), the howl breaks up and out until

I seem to be melting into the oncoming night and torrential rain. I'm ecstatic with grief, oblivious to the street.

The traffic lights turn red. A silver Toyota stops, and the driver rolls down the window.

'You all right, love?' I recognise the hot-chocolate man. Headlights twinkle on the gutter. I gulp. The howl is angry to be interrupted. It is far too soon.

'Yes.' The lie hurts, my ears ring as if I'm a diver surfacing with the bends. Realising I may need an excuse, I add, 'I was just in the hospital.'

'Me too. Where do you need to get to? I'll give you a lift.'

I drop weakly into the passenger seat, and buckle up. His car smells of Opal Fruits.

The lights change. A vague memory of normal behaviour prompts me to ask: *What do you do?*

'At the moment, I'm looking after my mam and dad. But usually I buy and sell things,' he says mysteriously.

'What sort of things?' I ask. Looking sideways, I notice he steers with one wrist on the wheel.

'Oh, vintage cigars, photographs, all sorts of stuff. I got started with conkers in the school playground. Used to soak them in vinegar so they were invincible weapons. I was making a killing. The head teacher announced in assembly: "Will the little boy who is selling conkers please stop it?" So I had to pack it in.'

'Fools,' I say. 'They should have put you in charge of the tuck shop.'

He drops me at the corner by the war memorial. Then, an after-thought, 'What's your name?'

I tell him.

'You can call me Sven,' he says, and drops a beat. 'Short for Svengali.' With a high yelp, the kind of laughter you hear from those who are desperate or deeply despairing, he hits the accelerator. I have a feeling that Sven and I are going to walk the same road for some time. But I will definitely not share his moccasins.

The definition of shock was unknown to me. I drifted through the days in a haze of bland apathy, missing deadlines, failing to answer emails. In her memoir of the aftermath of her son's death, *Time Lived, Without Its Flow*, poet Denise Riley writes of grief as a rupture, 'this curious sense of being pulled right outside of time, as if beached in a clear light'. To resist those tides of timelessness I kept a new timetable saved on my desktop, so I could track Anna's relentless schedule in rehab. Physio to help with mobility, and other activities to adapt to reduced mobility. Craft. Speech and Language Therapy. (Someone who had often told me of the thrills of simultaneous interpreting, Anna now seemed to be interpreting herself, reaching deep within to slowly excavate a language no one else knew.) Understanding Your Stroke, a course to build empowerment and autonomy. After a few weeks, Understanding Your Stroke disappeared. 'Why?' I ask. 'Did you graduate?'

'It was rubbish. The psychologist he. She was rubbish. I did not wish to do it.'

I laugh at Anna's characteristic hauteur, unchanged by stroke. Thirty minutes of someone lecturing you on your brain injury might indeed be more tedious than the daytime television on the ward.

We sit side by side on her bed. The foam mattress sighs when I settle on to it. Over the winter I've got used to hospital beds, articulated like model dinosaurs, their surprise elevations at a button's touch. For a few months, the nurses locked the sides of the bed to prevent Anna falling out. It is a relief when these barricades – and other safeguards against everything going wrong – start to come down.

We run out of things to say quite quickly. We had so very little to say to each other before, and now that there's such an enormous event to discuss, there are no words. We never held much store in chit-chat. Besides, Anna gets so tired, and I get so distressed.

Therefore, we only say essential things.

Today I am beating around the essential thing, the thing I'd hoped to discuss in different circumstances months ago – that I consider our relationship over, but I am still here, on her team. I meant to tell her last time, and the time before that. I didn't have the courage. And I was wary in case the news might affect her recovery. I cannot procrastinate any longer. Now even the kind doctors are asking about The Future. Is our flat adaptable? I point out that we don't own our flat. We can barely cover the rent, let alone make improvements, if the landlords allowed us to do so. The kind doctors seem surprised to be faced with a couple so unsettled and impoverished and I feel a gnawing sense that I have not done life right, not at all.

Now it looks as though I am going to do it even less right, by casting an explosive device into the midst of Anna's recovery. But I cannot hide from my heart. I believe in telling the truth, even a hard truth – especially to the people I'm closest to, who are inevitably those I will hurt most. Duplicity is too insulting. When the truth is told, everyone can share equally in a story. As I voice my doubts, I realise that, of course, Anna has long had her own.

'Yes,' she says, with a faraway look. 'We just missed our window.'

She takes my hand and squeezes it, hard. There is a long silence.

'Well, I'll go now,' I say.

'I'll see you out.'

'No really, it's okay.' I know what a palaver getting into the wheelchair is, and she needs that energy for other things. Anyway, the wheelchair seems to have disappeared. Another problem to solve. I will ask the nurse.

By way of answer she swings her legs heavily off the bed, first the left, and then the right. Slowly she eases her feet onto the ground, as if unsure that it is really there. Slowly she shifts her weight forwards, until both feet bear her up. She is standing.

My exhausted heart wrenches again. To see someone who has been prone for months stand independently upright is like a remembered piece of music. The music is uplifting, and also slightly ominous – a Wagner overture perhaps. I'm afraid Anna will fall, and if she falls, she can't reach out to brace herself. The sight seems to contravene and confuse all concepts of space, as when you look at your surroundings from upside down or try to cut your own hair in a mirror. Surely our positions are somehow reversed, and I've been laid flat out on the floor.

'Come on then,' she says.

And with not a little pride she lifts her right foot and places it down gently, and then her left, and she is walking. Her concentration as intense as that of an astronaut, removed from the gravity of a familiar planet. Astronauts train for years to enter space, but descent is different hurdle altogether. 'Returning to Earth brings with it a great sense of heaviness,' wrote Buzz Aldrin, describing his life after the first moon voyage, 'and a need for careful movement.' Beside me, slowly, heavily, in her baggy leggings, down the blue linoleum corridor to the doors that lead into the winter night – and to our flat, and my train to Brussels, to the reading at the Literaturhaus. We

II

move side by side, and despite now being severed, at last, being more separate than we've been for a decade, we are still so close that I sense each impending trip, feel in my own body the efforts Anna makes to correct her balance. Balance is the ongoing repair of the body's endless falling. The rawness of our (now, at last) shared anguish is an odd bond in an environment where drugs and television are provided to minimise pain. At the nurse's station we pause and she leans on my arm for a few seconds.

'Hello, Anna, making a run for it?' says the nurse.

'Please can you let Nancy out?' she says with dignity. The security doors can only be opened by staff.

The door sighs shut behind me and I look back through the small squares of wire-reinforced glass. Anna stands in the corridor of the institution that has been her home for some months now, looking after me. We pause, separated by the grid. Then, lifting her right leg as if a great weight is tethered to it, and setting it down, she turns and begins the long journey back to her room.

'It's easy to find, just drive through the main entrance and take a right after the giant sunflowers.'

I always gave pedantic directions when booking the taxi, but drivers still got lost in the hospital grounds. As the date of Anna's discharge approached, she sometimes spent an afternoon at the flat, so she could practise Living at Home. (It was a terrifying prospect; the physiotherapists were bombarding Anna with questions about the safety of steps and showers.) I'd await a phone call from an irritated taxi driver, implying the Centre for Enablement and Spasticity Clinic did not exist.

As we waited by the hospital entrance one afternoon Anna

asked if I would continue to live with her for one more year, but now as her primary carer. 'I can't do this alone,' she said.

What had happened to The Future? I'd been too preoccupied with keeping the howl in check to make any plans at all. As the black saloon cruised through the drab streets behind the golf course, I made my decision. In honour of our former conspiracy, I said yes.

In Germany I pack my books into boxes. I return to Oxford via readings in Barcelona and Madrid, travelling across a frightened Europe as the first cases of Covid are confirmed. At each airport I can feel border doors slamming behind me. It's raining at Heathrow. The coach speeds down the M40 and through the Stokenchurch Gap, the grand chasm in the steep chalk cliffs that opens onto the Vale of the White Horse. The crumbling white walls of 88-million-year-old stone pass in a blur, and ahead lie the wide fields and low hedges of Oxfordshire, the outline of the Wittenham Clumps, above which cumulous clouds gather, and a horizon disappearing west towards Wales. The coach rolls down Headington Hill, under chestnut trees bursting into spring green. I walk the final mile along the Iffley Road and past the Greyfriars, my suitcase rumbling through puddles behind me. The hipster baker who keeps irregular hours is closing for the night. He's left a crate of unsold sourdough baguettes on the pavement with a handwritten sign: *Help yourself.* I do. Bread and salt, the symbols of housewarming across so many cultures. A welcome-home gift. Maybe everything is going to be all right.

Who was I kidding? I unlock the front door, and find our corridor under an inch of sewage.

Anna was discharged a few days before lockdown. Due to the pandemic all outpatient therapies were written off, and her support worker was not permitted to visit. The Stroke Association hotline was silent. After living on the ward for months, she was suddenly alone. We were suddenly alone.

The first weeks were terrifying. Anna smashed every single glass we owned, she put pizzas in the oven still on their polystyrene bases, and pulled up the tulip bulbs I had planted in pots on the patio. Everything was a weed to her. One evening I heard a squeak in the other room, then silence. I rushed through to find her standing holding the curtain. It was in flames. I snatched it off the rails, bundled it up into a ball, doused it in the washing-up bowl. That night, I worried about sparks moving under the carpet, spreading secretly through the apartment and trapping us in an inferno.

It was not really a flat for the uncoupled, and despite Anna's generous offer I didn't think it would work to continue to share a bed. I pulled a bookcase out at an angle from the wall by the kitchen to make a private corner, and threw some blankets down on the tiles. From this perspective, before I fell asleep, I could see black mould creeping over the skirting board. The mould was a souvenir of the sewage. Like a bad conscience, every time I wiped it away, it returned.

I established a routine, unaware that it would continue for months: qi gong each morning, moving as much of our bodies as we could; then meals, equally slow and sombre. Anna had arrived home in a taxi, with a bin bag containing her clothes, and two wooden objects she had made in Craft: a birdhouse and a chopping board. The latter was a kitchen aid for her one-handed future. A spike extruded ferociously from one corner, to keep vegetables in place under the knife. Anna had hero-worshipped the debonair food writer Michael Ruhlman, but now she turned to the example of Michelin-starred chef Michael Caines, who lost his right hand in a car accident. She set out to learn to cook again, and spent hours meticulously chopping onions and leeks pinioned on the spike. These efforts were grimly rewarded; silent tears accompanied dishes to the table, the plates soon pushed away, our appetites gone.

Cherry trees blossomed and the avenues grew greener. Children painted rainbows in windows facing the street. It did not rain.

Questions arose: Can a paralysed limb feel pain? Where did those new bruises keep coming from, and should we tell someone? The changes to Anna's body were apparent, but what scribbled stars were shooting through her mind?

Ambulance sirens sounded more frequent but further away. The ice-cream van twinkled round its flat lure every day. People began to talk of *things not ever going back to normal*.

I read Anna's discharge letter. Perhaps it would have some answers. After several pages listing the physical repercussions of the stroke, it crashed to a conclusion with 'cognitive assessment'. 'In comparison to the patient's estimated pre-morbid functioning, the results indicated changes to aspects of memory, processing speed, abstract reasoning, and flexibility of thinking. The results were fed back to the patient, but she had difficulty coming to terms that some changes had occurred.'

Some stroke survivors experience lability – intense emotional reactions, such as laughing or crying. The word labile comes from Latin *labilis* to fall and, yes, there was a vertigo about Anna's uncontrollable weeping. She seemed to have drifted very far away. I felt unmoored, not knowing whether the tears were a true reflection of her psychological state or if she was experiencing a disruption in her brain's neural network. Either way, I felt powerless. When someone is crying in another room, you hear only the middle pitch of the agony, not the silent shudders and the tired ebbs of emotion. Anna's sharp howls were punctuated by a long silence each side that I knew was beyond solace.

As if degrees of weeping were a shared line of communication, the slightest setback sent me into a maelstrom too. I tried to hide my distress from Anna, but every night, after she'd gone to sleep, I wriggled down into my sleeping bag behind the bookcase and wept.

In the bathroom, I take Anna's right arm lightly in my own and ease it away from her side. This is her dominant hand, also once commonly found holding a cigarette, sharpening a Blackwing pencil, balancing a Sabatier knife, stroking a keypad. This is the hand she fucked me with. Her fingers now have an instinctive resistance to me that the rest of her body has never demonstrated. They curl back when I touch her. This is how I discover that paralysis does not mean no movement. Anna has made an excellent fist. But a fist is not what is needed now.

I swizzle the lever on the silver nail clippers, and prise her little finger straight. An iron fist: she winces. Three swift clicks to pare down the pale lacuna. She inhales sharply. I'm nervous about cutting her. The skin is too soft: a velvet glove. These nails are thicker than those on her left hand, as if grown with greater concentration. I work along the nails, scraping musty gunk out from under them. We're all being told to wash our hands more often, but Anna is definitely not doing so. How to wash your hands with one hand? Like the old joke about silent applause. Was it even a joke? I can't remember.

Anna lowers her right hand gingerly into the sink by holding it in her left as if it is strange to her, and gasps when it hits the luke-warm water. Her arm has grown so thin. I soap my own hands and swoosh them around hers, holding them in mine as I did in former times.

Day blurs into day. The nights grow longer again. I begin to see a therapist. It offers a more companionable way of weeping. We talk of alchemy, and what is underneath the dross. I wake myself in the night to write down my dreams. I dream the world has been taken over by a pandemic. The fact of living through a pandemic seems so implausible that I disbelieve the dream even as I dream it, but when I wake it is the only aspect of the dream true to reality.

Reality becomes virtual and moves online to smaller and smaller screens, and work becomes streams and threads and scrolls from which people can never go home – people are already at home. And they stay at home, unless they are in hospital – and there are more people in the hospitals than the hospitals can hold.

Sometimes our neighbours bang pans in the street. Soon it will be a new year. I am really looking forward to ringing out the old one. I order a bottle of good red wine, and we plan a feast that would not disgrace the repeat episodes of *Floyd on France* we've been watching. On the last morning of 2020 I take Anna her coffee and toast as usual. I double-take at the sight of what is in the bed.

'It's worse than it looks.'

'Oh my god. Do you mean it's not as bad as it looks?'

'No. I mean, yes.'

Anna's hair is matted to her skull, her face is smeared with blood. There are streaks of blood across the floor. Her left eye is blackened and puffy and is not looking at me. At least she is able to sit up.

'What on earth happened?'

'I think I fainted. I'm fine.'

'I'm sure you're fine, but we should get someone to check everything out. Especially as tomorrow is a holiday.'

I call for medical advice, on the smartphone that is increasingly my only connection with The World. Anna's coffee goes cold as we sit side by side, answering the routine questions. Are you bleeding? Are you in pain? Anna looks exasperated. She is always in pain.

'Can you get yourself to hospital?' asks the operator.

'Well . . .' says Anna.

'No,' I say firmly.

I wash the blood from her hair, rinsing again and again with a teacup until the water swirling down the sink runs clear. Just in time. A top-notch ambulance team arrives and whisks Anna away to A&E. Late in the evening she is escorted home with stitches in her eyebrow and a new diagnosis to add to her collection: a fractured zygomatic bone. New year, new scars.

A friend sends me a parcel. Inside the brown paper is a little square of striped linen tied with string and, inside that, two heads of dried yarrow. The minuscule star-shaped flowers are light pink on one sprig, on the other dusty white. Sarah writes that she found the yarrow growing among the grass on a Neolithic tomb in Scotland. Now, on my short daily walk down to the Thames, I notice yarrow everywhere in hedges and verges. It is a plant of visions: the stalks are scattered to tell the I Ching; applied to the eyelids, it is said to bring sixth sight. The Ancient Greeks believed Chiron the centaur once taught Achilles its use as a balm for wounds; it was rumoured to originate not from pollen but the particles of rust he scraped from his spear during the Trojan War. The botanical name *Achillea millefolium* translates as 'Achilles' thousand-leaved herb' but it is also known as woundwort, nosebleed plant (it starts and stops them), old man's pepper, devil's nettle, sanguinary, thousand-leaf and thousand-seal, bloodwort, *herbe militaris*, knight's milfoil. Starlings line their nests with the leaves, and lovers should place them under their pillow to bring good fortune.

Even in the most cramped and temporary city digs I have tried to find a means of growing things. Now iridescent bulbs hover in hourglass jars on our windowsill, catching the winter light, sending their roots swirling down into the waters below. A surprise effusion of blue and white to scent the warm room. Watching the hyacinths grow, knowing yarrow is hidden in my pocket, my anxiety diminishes. We are lucky to have outdoor space, a shady backyard, but the landlords have conspired to cover every inch of soil with gravel or concrete. This doesn't dissuade me. I order narcissus and snowdrop bulbs, and bury them in yoghurt cartons. In spring when the days start to lengthen I plant lettuce seeds in egg boxes, placing each seed gently a few millimetres away from the next. Distancing.

Two weeks later, tiny leaves sprout from the compost.

I post on social media asking for advice on assembling the grow-home. It was one of Anna's last purchases before her stroke, and I can't find the instructions. The many hollow metal struts that somehow interlock and hold up the plastic canopy lie in a heap on the paving slabs, like a game of giant Jenga. I have no opponent, and I never do discover how to slot them into place. I transplant the seedlings to a window box: this offers less protection from the elements than a grow-home, but I hope for the best.

A family of foxes digs an earth in the scrubland beyond the fence. The goldfinches and sparrows and the fox with half a tail are our only companions.

At night I am woken by our neighbour's garage light, which flickers on every time a wild creature passes. It stays lit for longer than any animal would linger, then there is darkness again.

The traditional lands of the Naskapi people are the tundra and forest of the Labrador coast. In winter they hunt caribou on the vast plains of the interior, but herds cannot feed where the snow becomes too deep or too firmly packed by the wind. They move on. Naskapi hunters traditionally use the scapular bone or shoulder blade of a caribou as a divination tool, a map to determine where to travel next.

First the hunter must dream of herds of caribou. This is encouraged through sweat bathing, and a mesmeric rhythm is established by drumming or rattle shaking to induce visions. The dreams are often vague regarding the location of the herd, and so on waking from the trance, the hunter consults a clean, dry caribou scapula. The bone is placed over a fire so that it cracks and scorches. These chance fissures are then 'read' to determine the location of caribou and the route to be followed towards them. Thus the hunt moves to new pastures rather than going over old, depleted territory.

Sometimes the scapula will give an answer the hunters do not wish to hear, but there are ways to circumvent the original augury, by performing further rituals. Sometimes, if the reader has incurred the spirits' wrath, the scapula lies.

I peel a ruby grapefruit and share out the segments between us.

'What do you want from life, hon?' I ask.

Anna looks as serious as the question demands, and says, 'I want to live with grace. It is hard to have grace now, but I will do my best.'

I struggle to keep my cool in the face of this devastating display of fortitude, and continue my questions as planned. 'Should we stay together? This arrangement seems to work okay.' I can't imagine any other life at present. But Anna is more practical.

'Yes. I mean no. We should live apart. You can visit me any time,' she adds kindly.

I don't have a scapula, but I have downloaded an I Ching app for my phone.

I ask it the same question, and the response comes back: THUNDER *over* THUNDER. *Poplar fluff, like snow. In winter the thunder sleeps beneath the earth. Now at the turning point it arises slowly. Know all movement is reinforced by rest. For the return to health after illness, look to the return to understanding. Only after estrangement will it come.*

We are listening to *Desert Island Discs*. An elderly etymologist is telling Lauren Laverne about his difficult childhood. The radio is a good preventive against tears. Today, lunch is tomato soup and half a bagel each.

Jewish mythology relates that in the womb the soul knows all the secrets of heaven, but at birth an angel presses a fingertip just above the child's lip, which seals each of us to silence. The impression of the angel's finger is lasting: it becomes the philtrum. Our faces bear the mark of all the knowledge we cannot express.

I see something in Anna's eyes I have missed, without realising it, for years. Clarity? The numbness of the stroke still haunts her face, but I sense her spirit is back. As the weeks pass, words are beginning to return too, although some days they all disappear again. The mercurial nature of her language reminds me of the changeable character of circumpolar shores in winter. On Baffin Bay the ice does not melt by gradual degrees but dances a jig with tides and weather: sometimes floes frozen solid can be safely crossed by a hunter's sled or a fishing expedition, sometimes fragments are blown out to sea by a storm, unveiling tidal deeps in which mussels and kelp grow. Anna's language is more colourful than before; she has a new specialty in idiom. Explaining how hard she finds it to spell a word, she says: 'I can manage three letters. Then it all heads south.'

I can almost believe she has fully recovered, until she says something so off-kilter it floors me, or the fridge is overtaken by a glutinous mess that takes me back to the worst of the old days. I recall how wary my friends in the Arctic were of making plans to cross the ice. I feel powerless to make plans now.

Our favourite exchange, once a day at least, goes like this:

'What are you thinking?' I am staring out the window at the rowan tree.

Sometimes I am thinking things I can't tell her. 'I was wondering what you were thinking?'

'I was thinking – oh, nothing much.'

The *What is Communication?* brochure could have been designed for any relationship: be patient, do not finish your partner's sentences, try to listen. Besides, there are forms of expression other than speech. After almost a decade together, often I understand where Anna's thoughts are heading, even when her words can't get there. Sometimes after a long pause, against the brochure's advice, I do suggest a word, and she looks relieved.

Living with another's aphasia makes me weigh my own words more carefully. I feel gluttonous, if I use too many. I turn down work, because I have nothing to say.

How do you talk about The Future, when the next word is elusive?

'Ask me tomorrow,' Anna says whenever she finds something inexpressible. Ask me tomorrow.

It was the hottest spring on record, again. People in the cul-de-sac next to the park set up distanced deckchairs in the road to chat with their neighbours. Anna had said I should wait for the first new flowers before leaving, and one morning I saw a glint of yellow in the neighbour's forsythia bush. The UK was still in its second lockdown, but it was time for me to move on.

Some aspects of the separation are painless.

'Can I keep one of your Moomin mugs?'

'Of course, which colour?'

'The red one.'

'The one with roses on?'

'Yes.'

In return, Anna gives me a stack of blank notebooks. 'I won't use them now,' she says.

I pack them in the bag I am preparing for the road. Nothing is certain but that I have too many books and too little money.

Sven phones when lockdown eases.

'How is Anna?'

'Okay. How is your dad?'

'Still alive.' Pause. 'How are *you* doing?'

I tell him. I tell him about the sewage and the broken grow-home and the falls and fractures and the silence and despair and that I'm trying to move on.

'You're a rubbish mate, as soon as things are hard you just clam up. You oughta talk to people about this shit sooner.'

'Okay. Supper?'

We arrange to meet at Polish Kitchen in the precinct. Alicja's small restaurant has forest decor: the walls are laminated floor to ceiling with photographs of beech trees, their intense viridian digitally enhanced. Now customers must sit at wooden picnic tables on the Astroturf outside. When Anna and I were regulars here, Alicja would bring us free vodka shots after the meal, and linger and chat. I order the special for Sven and me: *bigos*, hunter's stew, with mash and beetroot slaw.

I thought the operation I've been running was challenging, but Sven's situation gives me a tougher perspective. Unwilling to put both his parents into care, he has converted the family house in a North Oxford crescent into a private care home: here he looks after his elderly father, his bedridden mother, and gives his vulnerable brother a secure environment – if a somewhat chaotic one.

'Our family, we're like that stuff the waves leave behind on the beach.'

'Jetsam?'

'Yeah. All the rotting seaweed and dead jellyfish and bits of old Lego . . . we're just hanging around, waiting to be washed away by the tide. Have you got somewhere to go?'

'I haven't decided. Maybe I'll head north.' A friend has offered me a bothy on the Isle of Mull. In moments of bravado I tell myself I've had enough of this landlocked county, this posh southern city, where I never felt at home anyway.

'I don't get it. What do you want with always moving from place to place? You need to settle down and get on with your life.'

'I'm a travel writer.'

'Alexander Fleming went on holiday for two weeks. He left his Petri dishes without cleaning them, and when he came back they were accumulating mould. It was only then, seeing the mould and the clear space around it, that he understood bacterial growth, which led him to discover penicillin. He said, "One sometimes finds what one is not looking for." He needed the stability of a lab to make that breakthrough. Take time out, by all means. But you need a place to come home to.'

'This is my chance to start again. It's a new chapter.' I do not wish to admit to Sven that I know how exhausting starting over elsewhere will be. But I can't afford to live solo in one of the most expensive cities in the UK, in which Anna and I survived only by pooling our resources and negotiating a series of peculiar housing arrangements with friends and relatives.

I'm talking more than I've talked all year. I've almost forgotten how to do this, the easy flow of unprompted conversation. I tell Sven about the times I've managed perfectly fine without anywhere to live. My first days in London after university, arriving to take up an internship with an independent publisher, an opportunity I was so grateful for that I didn't mind that the only payment was a monthly travel card. I got the full zone usage out of that card. For a few weeks I sofa-surfed, getting to know the capital from Stratford to St John's Wood, then when I felt embarrassed to ask friends any longer, I slumped into the back seat on buses, the one on the right-hand side over the warmth of the engine, or snatched a couple of hours' sleep in station toilet cubicles; the nights were long but not without character and in a city you can blend into people just coming home or setting off to work. In the office, the Excel spreadsheets grew blurry as I caught up on sleep. To sleep securely, I got myself locked into parks; I discovered cemeteries. Cemeteries sometimes had toilets. It was not the roughness of sleeping rough that I minded – that could be covered up by a discreet wash in the sink at the publisher's office – but the fragmentary effect on the self of constant moving around. This society is not kind to those whose lives are organised around endless movement, although it's an ancient human instinct. I left my possessions with various friends, and soon forgot what I had left where, and later, what I had even owned to begin with. Within a few months, I had given up on a publishing career. One afternoon, I was browsing in a second-hand bookshop on the Charing Cross Road and the owner offered me a job. That's not quite true. I was browsing in a second-hand bookshop on the Charing Cross Road, when a young bookseller ran out from the back office in tears. The red-cheeked owner followed her as far as the shop door, shrugged, and turned to me.

'Do you want a job?'

The wages were just enough to make the rent of a bedsit in Highbury. I soon learned why my predecessor had left.

'That's why I went to Greenland,' I say to Sven. 'I was offered a log cabin on an island, in exchange for writing a book. It just seemed too good to be true to have a home of my own, even if I had to go to the Arctic for it.'

'Well, you can't go back to the Arctic now. You can't go anywhere in a pandemic. It's not safe.' Sven took a sip of his beer. 'You could live in our summerhouse. I could dolly it up a bit.'

He shows me a photo of the summerhouse on his phone. The traditional wooden kayaks he makes by hand are propped up in one corner, and there are large glass windows through which I can watch the grebe dive on the lake – and through which the neighbours can see in.

'That's really kind, but I'd need something a bit more private.'

'Well then, here's another idea. I've got some friends down by the canal. They live on a boat. Crazy!' he laughs.

You are crazy, I think. 'What's wrong with living on a boat?'

'You're as bad as they are. How do I get mixed up with these weirdos? Anyway, they're looking for someone to keep an eye on things down there. Probably right up your street.'

'Like *The Night Manager*?' I ask.

'Yeah, kind of. Bit less glamorous. Want to take a look?'

AFTERMATH

JUNE

*'Because a thing is going strong now, it need not go strong for
ever,' [Margaret] said. 'This craze for motion has only set in
during the last hundred years. It may be followed by a civilisation
that won't be a movement, because it will rest on the earth.'*

E. M. FORSTER
HOWARDS END

Tuesday 1 June

After lockdown, every encounter is piquant. Last night over take-away chow mein I encouraged Sven to tell me more about his friends, Aislin and the assassin. (*'What do they do?'*)

'Well,' he says. 'The assassin is called the assassin because that's what he was, a paramilitary, but he's not any more, he came to this country a wanted man, a freedom fighter. Now he's a Buddhist, sort of. Aislin studied physiology at Oxford – she's a genius. Long ago she abandoned Western medicine and began looking for new ways to heal people.

'You'll like them and they'll like you – but be careful. Don't get on the wrong side of them. As the Spanish say of the Gallegos: when you meet them on the stairs, you can't tell whether they're going up or coming down.'

However you decide to approach this slip of land between the rails and the canal, from east or west, a crossing has to be made. The rail bridge is one of the highest arches in the city: from it you can see every single spire. But if you come from the east, across the waters of the canal, there's only a little lift bridge. Its wooden boards tremble *clunk clunk* as Sven drives over. My heart is in my mouth.

The assassin is waiting at the gate to the woods. He tugs back an awkward bolt and leads us down a path scattered with white willow seeds. I recall the I Ching. *Poplar fluff, like snow.* At the fringes of the wood there's a glade, sheltered by three mature willows and hidden from the canal by bulwarks of brambles.

'That would be a good spot to moor a caravan,' he says. I look across the sea of nettles, in which hemlock umbels cast wavering shadows. An eerie scream pierces the morning air. A Great Western

33

train rips past the iron fence that borders one side of the woodland, shaking the wild hops twining up its spikes. The backdraught cools my face.

The assassin waits for silence. 'You'll have to clear the nettles.'

'It's a jungle,' says Sven. 'It will take a napalm strike to clear this.'

'Well, you could have a boat, if you like. I've got a narrowboat for sale.'

Rain starts to fall. A distant jangle of chains as the lift bridge rises to let a boat pass. The railway track and the canal must have been laid down around the same time, both built to power the metamorphoses of the Industrial Revolution. The woods have grown up between them, a sliver of stasis among the quest for commerce and speed.

'I can't afford a boat,' I tell him. A decision needs to be made. Sun breaks through the clouds and every leaf sparkles for a moment. Rain and sun come together only on a fox's birthday, the saying goes. 'I'll get a van and moor it here.'

Sven drives me back to his place. He is catastrophic. 'Oh man, what have we done? Even the junkies couldn't handle that dump. You're totally isolated. It's not safe. You could die out there and no one would find your body for days. You . . .'

'Relax. I'll be fine,' I say. 'I've survived much worse than this.'

We browse second-hand caravans on eBay. I prefer the older models. 'Look at those paisley cushions.'

'But it doesn't have a toilet!'

'I don't need a toilet.'

'Don't be an idiot. You'll be miles from civilisation. You need a toilet. Here's one. It's a four-berth. Do you want two-berth or four-berth?'

'I want something compact yet well designed.'

'A two-berth has a sofa that converts into a bed. A four-berth has a whole separate room. You ought to get a four-berth.'

'I don't want it to be ostentatious. I want it to look like a worthless heap of junk. I'm going to let the lichen grow over it so nobody knows it is there.'

'The two-berth ones are tiny,' he grumbles. 'You'll have no space.'

'I've had my Bavarian palace,' I say ruefully. 'My nights at the Savoy and the Algonquin.'

'Well, you're a nutter. But I get it. So long as the van is dry that's the main thing. The problem with these vintage vans is they are basic. I remember them as a kid back in Wales. They had no facilities because you parked them at a campsite and used the showers and stuff there.'

On closer investigation many of the vintage caravans are not just basic, they are burned-out, mouldering wrecks described as 'good restoration projects'. Those that have been refurbished are blighted by bunting and floral curtains. I set my heart on a tiny blue van, round as a button, but it is currently on the Isle of Skye ('owner will not deliver'). Then I discover the Alpine Sprite, a brand that promised the charm of Europe's summits, though the vehicles were more likely to be found at Pease Bay or on Canvey Island than up a snow-clad massif. Holidaymakers demanded more amenities as the summers passed, and so caravan interiors show subtle variations in layout. Does it matter whether the kitchen is at the end of the van, or in the middle?

'Hmm. Not sure I like the sound of that "cracked and sealed skylight". How about this one?'

I consider bidding £500 for an Alpine Sprite surrounded by daffodil fields in deepest Norfolk, but the owner needs payment in cash the next day.

'Stop being taken in by the fancy photos, dumbass,' Sven says. 'Take a look at this.' He points to a beige caravan parked in a suburban drive. We scroll through an image reel of bathroom fixtures in sage green Bakelite, complete with matching tooth mug, and the fold-out wood-veneer shelves in the kitchenette.

It's not a Sprite, it's a Buccaneer. I think of Paul Celan: 'a poet is a pirate'. The five-star seller gives an exhaustive list of the vehicle's qualities. *Must See!!! Double glazing!!! Quality Tyres!!! Aquaroll!!! Royale Porta-Potti (chemicals included)!!! Exellent power in hot shower!!! Curtains all Lovley and Clean!!!*

'Look, Sven. It's got a shower.'

'*One former owner, has to retire from caravanning being in his 90s,*' he reads. 'Aww. *Stored indoors, good damp rating.* Well. Sounds all right. Where is it?'

'Hither Green . . . that's south London. *No Time Wasters. This was a top spec model back in its day, please do bare in mind its 37 years old and does have some small minor marks.* Should we investigate the minor marks?'

'No time,' says Sven. 'The auction ends tomorrow. It's this one. Shit or bust.'

The current bid is £658. I raise it to £750. This is more than I have in my bank account. But it's less than a month's rent on the flat. And I soon won't be able to afford that either.

Wednesday 2 June

I'm woken by my phone ringing.

'*Alhamdulillah!*' Sven has been taking Arabic classes for three years. One day, when the pandemic is over, he will travel to the Rub' al Khali – the Empty Quarter – with his camera and take photographs of the dunes. '*Alhamdulillah! Hosanna! Mazel Tov!* You have a caravan. Drag your sorry ass down to the canal and clear those nettles.'

I tug back the bolt on the gate and walk down the lane with a rush of freedom. After months of matching my steps carefully to another's, I'm finding my own pace again. In the glade, spring is burgeoning into summer. Ivy scrambles up the trunks of alder and elder and ash, dressing the woods in uniform green. As I hack at the nettles with a blunt pair of garden shears, I consider my original plan to leave Oxford. Was it so absurd? I'm fond of this city, for all the lofty arrogance I've encountered at its academic heart. Even that cold core has its cosy spots. I recall the pub snugs once frequented by Iris Murdoch or J. R. R. Tolkien, spirits who trod the line between the university's strictures and the wild spaces of their own imaginations. Philip Pullman's description of Oxford in *The Subtle Knife* as a place where rifts in the fabric of this world might lead us into other worlds is not far from my own experience. I've found kindred spirits here, real and imaginary. I've speculated like Lyra with her alethiometer, trying to scry out some kind of future in dark times. I've meandered through unfamiliar neighbourhoods, discovering handy treasures: boxes of windfalls at the back gates of a convent, or jars of honey with a hopeful honesty box down a lavender path. Over the low walls of the most unkempt and mysterious front gardens I've browsed trestle tables exhibiting ('free to a good home') cuttings of saxifrage and sempervivums, miniature botanical gardens that hint at an orderly greenhouse hidden somewhere beyond the climbing roses and apple trees hung with Tibetan prayer flags. The main roads of the city branch out like the spokes of a mandala and between them run forgotten alleyways: Cuckoo Lane in the east, Jackdaw Lane in the south. Yet this threshold is the most distinctive one I've ever crossed.

Soon my gloves are caked with sweat and earth, and stiff as gauntlets. My body leans into the pleasure of labour again after months cramped indoors. *The earth shows up those of value and those who are good for nothing.* An ancient peasant judgement, recorded by John Berger: I'm making myself good for something. But what?

An old white dog with a wall eye appears, and sniffs silently among the nettles. I've seen this dog before. The assassin arrives soon after. He's come to see how I'm getting on. To check up on me? He is curt, but then I am short with him. Although speech is brief, this is a friendly visit. He brings an old scythe with a polished steel blade, which is more efficient than the garden shears.

Aislin and the assassin have been here twenty years. Yes, the land has changed in that time. Once this part of the canal was known as the Gates of Hell. It was much rougher then, he says, just a tip for the railway, with bonfires burning day and night. Junkies came to this patch, since the police never dared follow them down here. You still find syringes lying around, so watch out for your wheels – you'll have to check the ground over if you're going to drive the caravan in. And then there were the hippies, he breathes contemptuously, gesturing to a naked Cindy doll, its legs splayed, in the fork of one of the willows. It has been crucified with a rusted nail through its plastic abdomen. The hippies, they were worse than the junkies, he says, university drop-outs who wanted to live on the land but couldn't be bothered to look after it or even themselves. He gets his penknife out and saws the doll in half, casting the hollow pink torso down into the nettles, then begins to work loose the nail. They nearly burned the woods down and you still find bits of plastic crap like this, old yoga mats and shisha pipe and lighters. The nail comes loose and he pockets it. They mess everything up and then they move on. There was a Macedonian guy living here last winter, don't know what happened to him.

He takes a few steps towards the path, then turns back. 'Before it was the Gates of Hell,' he says, 'it was Joy's Field – I've seen the old deeds. It was named Joy after the farmer who owned the land before the railway took it, and you'll make it that again if you choose.'

I go back over the ground, the mown nettles wilting already in the noon heat, looking for debris. The assassin was right. Not only syringes, but bottles buried deep in the earth, bleary with condensation or ancient dried-up fermentation, and colourful fragments of foam that might once have been yoga mats. Most unnerving are the plastic bags: clagged with soil, hard to excavate, each time one comes to the surface I pray there is nothing sinister inside it.

I'm writing this slumped back against the willow, slugging water from a flask. My mind has not dwelt on anything painful all day, and I've just cleared enough ground to live on.

Thursday 3 June

I take Anna her morning mug of coffee. I wash the bin juice off the bin, put in a new bin liner, and uproot the chest-high fennel plant in the yard because Anna is disturbed by the feathery disorderliness of its leaves. (Since the stroke, she craves the reassurance of order.) I make banana bread, using up the self-raising flour that passed its best-before date three years ago.

'I don't like banana bread,' Anna says.

This is another world to the woods and the canal. I exist between places again – but rather than being impatient to settle, I realise how natural this double life feels to me. The captivity of the flat is not absolute, now I have appropriated a glade. The infinity of lockdown is ticking down. I catch Anna looking at me softly, as if she's trying to hold the moment in her memory. She says she will miss me, but I wonder if it is really me she will miss – or a connection with what we have been for each other. We are a trusted vault for each other's stories.

Sven is driving to Hither Green to collect the caravan. I ask him whether he likes banana bread.

He makes a disgusted face.

I can't accompany him. I have another engagement. The hair salon reopened a few weeks ago, and appointments are like gold dust.

'Can you cut it a bit shorter? I may not be able to wash it so often.' I tell Tia about Sven and the caravan.

'Oh, how gorgeous! Where will you take this caravan? To the seaside?'

'I can't drive,' I tell her. 'I'm just going to live in it.'

Tia laughs so much she has to put down the clippers. For the first time, I appreciate the situation might be a little surreal. I have a house on wheels, but I am unable to drive. I own my own home, but I don't have an address.

❋

I make a simple supper of pasta with a salmon and sage sauce, and Anna and I watch *The Lighthouse*, a film about two men stuck on a remote skerry in a storm. There is little dialogue, but lots of howling wind, inaudible mutterings over biblical texts, neurosis, ghosts, and an increasingly hopeless wait for rescue. At the end, there is one man left and a corpse is swinging from the weather station.

Friday 4 June

I loved you, so I drew these tides of men into my hands
and wrote my will across the sky in stars
to gain you Freedom, the seven-pillared worthy house . . .
T. E. Lawrence

Although we officially separated over a year ago, physically leaving has been hard to orchestrate, and it still feels like a betrayal. (I remind myself this is a mutual agreement. That I stayed far longer than I ever intended.) In twenty minutes Sven will arrive in his bashed-up Luton. I will be free (I think) of the strain that has eaten away at me for the last year, the doubts and anxieties that beset every moment. In the last minutes of our decade together Anna and I sit on the sofa. This is the *Sidet' na chemodanakh* or 'sitting on suitcases', a pause before going on a journey, a family tradition she adopted on her own travels, and taught me to anchor mine.

I say, 'Well, it's time.'

She squeezes my right hand in her left.

'I wanted to order *The T. E. Lawrence Poems* for me. I mean you,' she says. Gwendolyn MacEwen's book was the first of hundreds she lent me.

'We can still share one copy between us,' I say. 'We have too many books and nowhere to put them.'

'I don't even know where it is.' She has given most of her books away.

'No. Well, it will be *somewhere*.'

I remember the day we visited the Dorset barn, Cloud's Hill, that Lawrence made his retreat when he returned from Damascus. Here he enjoyed 'an almost unbroken peace'. The house was certainly not seven-pillared, as Anna and I discovered after our high-spirited drive down the A34 on a sunny morning in our first year together. Even so, it held distinct rooms: a book-lined library; a spartan bunk-room lined with tin foil, like a child's concept of a rocket to blast into outer space. On the lintel Lawrence had carved words from a text by Herodotus: *ou phrontis*, 'don't worry'.

The doorbell rings. I am keeping back tears; it is Anna who is able to speak.

'You have done an immense thing. Now bugger off.'

And so we begin our new and various solitudes.

There is no place for wistful nostalgia in Sven's world. He rolls down the back grate for my boxes: 'Aren't you lucky you know someone with a big truck?'

Although it takes only six minutes, the Buccaneer's voyage from Sven's driveway to the woods is epic. The caravan veers over the roundabout, and nearly drifts off the towbar under the Cassington bus. A lorry overtakes us. On its side: *Pukka Pies: Are you a Perfectionist? Don't Compromise!* Seconds later, we're off the main road and navigating the track to the canal. Clouds of cow parsley brush the sides of the van, as if it's an aircraft taking off into altitude. Potholes cause heavy turbulence. The van lurches round a bend, then bounces over the wooden lift bridge. *Clunk clunk.* The Canal and River Trust has pinned a sign on the bridge since my last visit. When I get out to open the gate, I go back to read it. *Unsafe for use.* Well, there's no need to drive the van back over – ever.

Even the most sophisticated vehicle can be hard to manoeuvre over rough terrain. Buccaneer wheels were designed for tarmac in Southend and Bexhill. Here, they stick in the boggy ground. Sven unhitches the van, while I lay down planks. Then we push, hoping the van will glide towards the centre of the glade. Will the thirty-seven-year-old axles survive? No movement. Three gongoozlers join us – we are better entertainment than the narrowboats. All five of us apply the full force of our bodies. Still no movement. The assassin turns up with a rope, one end of which he ties to the van; the other, he runs around the trunk of the largest willow. Using the tree as a lever, he pulls. Sven and I push and grunt. The van moves a millimetre forwards, then slips back. The assassin gives a tremendous heave, Sven and I rock the grab handles to get some momentum – and at last it lollops forwards several feet, and lands parallel to the railway fence.

Sven is filming everything on his GoPro.

'We don't want to forget this,' he says, waving the tiny video camera like a Fool's bauble in the Tarot.

I don't want the caravan on YouTube. He should be focusing on manoeuvres. 'Put away the toy!'

'I've been on grade-five rapids with this in my hand,' Sven says. 'Don't worry about it.'

The assassin lures Sven to his shed for a mug of tea. I haul my ruck-sack out the boot and dump it by the willow. When their voices have faded through the trees, I open the van door and step inside. The walls are thin as a Kinder Egg. There's just enough space to stand up in the galley, looking down between the two berths to the windows that wrap the front of the vehicle. I know the shelves will fill up with books and belongings and things from the woods. But now there is just one object I want to carry inside.

In the Scottish tradition of 'first-footing' the morning after Hogmanay, a visitor brings a lump of coal for good luck. In the pocket of my jeans I've hidden a small stone with a story as old as coal. During my own lifetime, it came to England from Denmark. I was working in an arts centre by the Limfjord, a deep channel forged by glaciers that runs west from the North Sea all the way across the peninsula to the Kattegat. The arts centre occupied a tower many storeys high which could be seen for miles in those watery flatlands. Off the spiral stairwell in the Education Room was a red wheelbarrow full of stones. How many thunderstones were in the wheelbarrow? None of the adults could remember, but busloads of children kept on guessing.

On Mors, the southern island in the Limfjord, these fossils are called *stjerne* after the five-pointed star that wraps the stone, and on the island of Als they are *kæmpeknap* or big buttons. Their name in English echoes the belief that they were forged at the spot where Thor's bolts of lightning hit the earth. In his *Natural History of Oxfordshire* (1677) Robert Plot writes that the stones '(by the vulgar at least) are thought to be sent to us from *inferior Heaven*, to be generated in the *clouds*, and discharged thence in the time of *thunder* and *violent showers*'. Thor was loved by peasants as a fierce

44

protector and because he commanded the weather that shaped their lives. A god of thunder and also of fertility. A force that promises the harvest's return, and defends wanderers from harm. The kind of deity that I need now.

It was believed lightning would not strike a house that held a thunderstone. And so they were placed on top of clocks, under floorboards, over stable doors. They were said to keep witches out of the dairy and bad dreams away from horses. Judging by the red wheelbarrow, such fossils were common in Jutland. And so, on my picturesque walks along the shores of the Limfjord, I looked for my own thunderstone, but it was weeks before I spotted one at last – and then, it was camouflaged among ballast at the side of a busy road. I closed my hand around the *stjerne*. It was a snug fit.

When I got back from Denmark, Anna revealed that she also possessed one of these fossils and during our years together, they sat next to each other on our bookshelves. But there are some storms that thunderstones cannot prevent.

I wondered whether to leave my stone alongside hers when I left. They had looked so good together, fitted so well. I hesitated, then pocketed it. Now I place it on the windowsill, the rows of dots that mark its surface gleaming like cat's eyes ahead of me on a dark road.

Saturday 5 June

Morag comes to share the first dinner I cook in the van. Whatever challenges lie ahead, one of my oldest friends is here to mark the new beginning. We grew up together in Northumberland, farther apart than most childhood friends but more distant still from any other kids. Years later, coincidentally we both found ourselves living in Oxfordshire – stunned by its narrow lanes and gentle seasons, its landscape lush but tame after the moors' austerity. This is our first meeting for over a year. She's supported her young family through lockdown; she's more than ready for a night off. I cook a rough ratatouille on the gas ring, throw in two bulbs of garlic and a chorizo sausage. Morag gets a couple of crates out of her boot for us to sit on.

As I raise the second forkful to my mouth, the ease of conversation with Morag, her kindness: it's all too much. Tensions slither from my muscles. My bones shiver and my stomach contorts. How dare my body exist outside that damp flat? How dare I feed it good things. How dare I leave someone who needed me. I lean back weakly against the shell of the van and breathe deeply to counter my nausea.

Dishes clatter companionably as Morag tidies away the stew: no point in prolonging a celebration that is painful. The sun sets over the railway tracks. A magpie hops between the sleepers like a hobo. The howl hasn't gone away. It has curled up and is resting, and will be all the stronger when it wakes. I can feel its weight in my abdomen. I wonder if it will seep away, as light is leaving the sky now, or change form. But not tonight, not soon. I realise with dread that this will be the work I do in the van, that grieving must take the place of other work for a while.

The noise in the galley quietens. Morag comes out to join me.

I remember another evening long ago – a ceilidh at her parents' farm. We escaped the furious reels and chains in the barn and walked out onto the silent moors. Flocks of sheep gleamed on the hills like constellations, making it hard to tell the dark skies from the dark turf. Fiddle notes echoing in our ears, we watched the skies for shooting stars and hints of the aurora from the far north. Here the only aurora is the ever-present orange glow of Oxford above the trees.

It doesn't quite obscure the stars. There's Betelgeuse, the red supergiant, one of the brightest stars in the night sky. Part of Orion, always the first constellation I seek out in the colder months. It orients me, wherever I am. When Orion rose over my cabin on the Upernavik archipelago, the figure the stars outlined was just one more hunter among the hunters who were my neighbours. But unlike those kind and generous men, the myth of Orion is a story of greed, and pertinent now as humans seem bent on destroying all the life systems on the planet.

The Ancient Greeks believed Orion was able to walk on water, perhaps because the constellation is most visible in winter, a time of stormy weather at sea. He was mortal, not a god at first, just a monster of a man, a giant, so strong that he could kill any animal, and he wanted women like trophies too, and so he got into trouble, taking his mother by force, among many others. His father blinded him, not for this but for watching the innocent sun as she rose in the east. Aurora, goddess of the dawn, had a soft spot for Orion, and she forgave him for peeping and gave him his sight back, and then of course he seduced her too, and Artemis, the huntress. He hunted not only the huntress but also her hare, and wilder beasts, and boasted he'd kill all the animals on earth, but before he could do so he was felled by a small scorpion hidden under a stone. He was too much for the gods, one of those who so revels in life they end up destroying themselves. But like fond parents, they could not bear his loss, so they kept him with them in the skies.

Immortality is relative. Now the constellation Orion is burning up too. Betelgeuse his right shoulder and Rigel his foot won't last more than another thousand years.

The light has gone. An owl calls.

Morag breaks the silence. 'Tawny,' she says.

Sunday 6 June

The van is a bazaar of all my belongings, a reindeer herders' *chum* smothered in hides. The fabric on the berth cushions has a pattern of autumn leaves, rather like a compost heap. I throw down sheepskins from Bavaria and woollen blankets from Iceland, bright silks from Marrakesh. Familiar softness, rescued from boxes to remind me of distant places and people I love. I buy a new duvet cover, new pillowcases. I hang my storm lantern over the window.

Soon all the shelves are bookshelves. The classic *Collins Bird Guide* comes to the van, along with older field guides I've collected, and activity books for children, such as *i-SPY Wildflowers*. Some, like *Stars at a Glance: a handy sky guide on novel lines* (1916), have been read so often the covers are falling off, the spherical celestial charts faded from blue to grey. There's something charming yet alarming about these publications dating from a time before wildlife was widely considered an indicator of climate change. Most come from second-hand shops, but there are relics from my own life too, including the first prize I ever won. My primary school had such small classes, our teachers must have decided to award prizes to all pupils rather than celebrating only a few high-achievers. I was given an illustrated guide to wild flowers, which I've treasured ever since; the artist has drawn each plant not in isolation but added glimpses of habitat, debris such as decaying leaves, pebbles and snail shells, like an old Dutch still-life painting. The certificate on the endpaper records that the book was awarded for 'quiet determination'. Only now do I realise the teachers must have concocted prizes specifically to match our talents.

I set aside the cocktail cabinet for favourite poets, and there's just enough room for a bottle of whisky too – so the cabinet bears a trace of its former use, and the poets have a libation.

There are limits to what the caravan can hold. I need to put some things into storage.

'How much more stuff do you have?' Sven asks. I tell him. He's incredulous. 'Can't you get rid of it?'

'But it's all my work, my books,' I say.

'What you need is a garage,' he says. 'You can rent a garage off the council for twenty quid a week. Or why not put them in our summerhouse?'

The cheapest place I can find (apart from the summerhouse) is a yard that rents out shipping containers down by Fiddler's Island, a desolate spot where a number of tributaries join the Thames.

Bookcases and boxes of books, drafts for past and future books, artwork – I'm wary of storing all this paper on the flood plain. These meadows were underwater most of last winter. But Richie is reassuring as he hands over the key: shipping containers are watertight, he says. They're designed to cross the ocean . . . I wrench the container doors shut on my life's work, and slam down the locking gear.

The copper key fob is in the shape of an old-fashioned diver's helmet. It reminds me of pictures I've seen of the deep-sea diving suit patented by Harry Houdini in 1921. Houdini never used the suit in his own performances, perhaps because its design was promoted as easy to escape from, while his reputation rested on danger and difficulty. Houdini is remembered as a magician, but his true art was escapology; he understood how to get out of a tight place. This involved not only knowledge of human anatomy, and a fine judgement of his own physical breaking point, but also of the paraphernalia in which he shrouded and enchained his body, only to dramatically free himself again. Publicity photographs show Houdini looking disarmingly slim and shy, locks arranged coyly over his long johns, chains like a second skin.

At night with the lantern lit and the velveteen pencil-pleat curtains drawn under the pelmet, the atmosphere in the van is expectant as a cinema before the film begins. Or – it's as louche as a vaudeville dressing-room, with tiny LED lights running round the windows like miniature versions of the bulbs on backstage mirrors. Above all the van is true to its name, a bootleg Buccaneer riding the high seas. This chamber could be the cabin of an officer or a first mate on a polar expedition – that is, one of those who slept in luxury surrounded by books and chronometers, and even a wardrobe to store their uniform with its polished brass buttons. Not here the musty communal hammocks of the crew.

It's cosy, but some of the windows have missing latches and can be easily lifted open from the outside. The window above the sink has an intractable blind. After midnight, the lights of a bicycle returning to a distant boat flicker across the ceiling. I'm curious about my new neighbours. I am the object of curiosity too. In the night I hear a rustle and the crack of a branch. Is it a heavy-stepping deer, or a human trying to step lightly? I lie awake, listening – but the visitor has gone.

Monday 7 June

Flames glided in the river, small green flames, red flames,
white flames, pursuing, overtaking, joining, crossing each other
– then separating slowly or hastily.
Joseph Conrad, *Heart of Darkness*

People are emerging from lockdown, like sleepy ladybirds when spring sun warms a windowpane. Word has got out about the caravan. Helen Mitchell sends a parcel from the Norfolk Broads, with coffee from Wilkinson's, her favourite roasters in Norwich. The writer C. C. O'Hanlon, who has spent the last year travelling across Europe with his wife Given, striving to stay ahead of immigration laws and bailiffs and the street itself, zips over a collection of useful e-books, including *The Camper Van Bible* and Jessica Bruder's *Nomadland*.

There's a bonfire party at the canal. Sparks flicker into the summer twilight and the cathartic heat blisters my skin. It's hard to believe I'm really here among people like Ariel, who seems to have hope without limits, a keenness to meet the world undimmed by grief.

Ariel lives on the long green boat, *Nordica*. She tells me she grew up in Suffolk in a shed her architect father built on the ruins of a former barn. He added doors and windows discarded from medieval churches, and fitted out the kitchen with parts of vintage caravans. The shed later became her studio. After this haphazard domesticity, a boat was the obvious step.

Ariel doesn't ask my reasons for moving into the van, and I'm grateful. Nor does she ask how long I'll stay. This tact characterises everyone I encounter here. Perhaps too many of us have stories that are painful, or just too complicated, to tell a stranger. Conversation stays in the present, with practical concerns, and does not dwell on the past. The traditional boaters' greeting 'howdo?' has been replaced by a more contemporary 'alright?' The blessing of both is their brevity, allowing an easy exchange as boats pass each other. No more answer is required than to repeat the greeting back.

Ariel explains that the moorings on this stretch of canal are known as Agenda 21, after a directive created at the Earth Summit in Rio in 1992 to encourage small groups to preserve their neighbourhoods. Agenda 21 was formed originally by a boaters' co-operative and British Waterways to establish ecological moorings for the narrowboats. Given the boaters' interest in their environment, the group has also protested against property development. The desire to resist never dies.

'Have fun in the van!' Ariel says, by way of farewell. I wonder at the word *fun*, it's been a while since that was in my lexicon. *Survival* has been the only objective.

The daunting but irresistible possibility of fun is coloured by a fresh awareness of Anna's pain, which I'd almost become inured to. I acclimatised to difficulty day after day in the confines of our flat; now, in a place with limited accessibility, each new experience doubles as a reminder of what she is missing. Yet these first encounters after liberation from lockdown are tinged with fear and uncertainty for everyone. We try to stand a safe distance apart, and can't quite hear each other.

Jack Lamb certainly can't hear me. He dribbles over with an alcohol-free beer, looking unwashed and under-slept. His wrinkled face is distorted by huge rimless glasses. 'Look,' he says, thrusting out a waxy white hand into the safe space between us. 'Dead man's finger.'

I've never heard Raynaud's disease described this way. I thought dead man's fingers were a kind of fungus. It's a conversation starter, anyway. They didn't have any bonfires last year, he tells me. Too many people dying.

I recognise his accent. 'Are you from Maine?'

'New Hampshire ... and most everywhere. I was a ride jock for the carny. So your boat, I mean van, where is it? Do you park or pitch it?' he asks.

'Maybe moor it?'

'How do you write poetry?' His questions ricochet through my isolation mind. 'Do you, uh, just wait for the right words?'

I tell him that sometimes writing is a canal and you have to work hard to dig a channel for the water to flow through, and crank the windlass to open the lock gates, and sometimes it comes swiftly as a river in spate that overflows its banks.

'Stay afloat! Be the cork, not the bottle.'

I leave long before the bonfire burns down, and walk back to the woods mulling over Jack's elliptical wisdom. The company of others feels overwhelming after so long in the basement. Small talk seems a kind of betrayal of Anna. The phatic conversations that are necessary when you meet new people fill me with a wild rage. Whereas Anna and I struggle to communicate, others are wasting their breath and cognitive skills on all this trivia. Their words overflow and flood my reduced capacity. Will I ever regain my equilibrium, stay afloat – and lighten up? One way to hide from the troubling thoughts kindled by such encounters is to wrap myself in unruffled solitude. But how will I ever recover, if I hide away? Perhaps this van that everyone seems to believe is a boat on land will carry me gently back into the world.

Tuesday 8 June

*Imagine the feelings of a commander of a fine . . . trireme in
the Mediterranean, ordered suddenly to the north . . . Imagine
him here – the very end of the world, a sea the colour of lead,
a sky the colour of smoke, a kind of ship about as rigid as a
concertina – and going up this river with stores, or orders, or
what you like. Sand banks, marshes, forests, savages, – precious
little to eat fit for a civilised man, nothing but Thames water
to drink.*

Joseph Conrad, *Heart of Darkness*

Stormy weather. Raindrops leak through the window. I lie on my
berth and read the copy of *Heart of Darkness* I picked up at the Little
Free Library on the canal.

Wednesday 9 June

A day for practicalities. The assassin is coming to help me level the
bed of the van. While I wait for him, I fill the Aquaroll (an ingenious
invention, like a small beer barrel, which makes transporting water
supplies easy) from the standpipe on the towpath.

A ginger cat is asleep in the sun on *Marmalade Stripe*'s roof.
Prerona, another acquaintance from the bonfire, is serving coffee to
two guests. Narrowboats are ideal for socially distanced meetings.
With a friend perching on a campstool on the other side of the
towpath, there's always a metre between bodies at least – or 'a llama
length' as Prerona's hand-painted sign politely reminds passers-by.

I roll back through the gate, and the bolt slams down on my
finger. The agony is intense.

The assassin arrives an hour later than promised. 'We keep relaxed time here.'

He looks at my swollen finger, 'Oh, that's nasty.' Rather than offer any first aid, he tells me that in many cultures, a wound to the hand or foot is a sign of luck in new ventures.

'Good choice of van.' He peers inside. The assassin used to have a business designing and constructing treehouses for rich families, but now he's building his own house in the woods. Caravans have more in common with treehouses than they do with ground dwellings. From the tree canopy you get a change of perspective, he says. Slight, yet significant. The same goes for a house on wheels, too – even though it may not be so high off the ground. A matter we're going to decide right now.

I'm glad of his advice as the caravan came with few instructions. I have got to grips with the Aquaroll and the PortaPotti, but the water heater is a mystery, and all the pipes . . . Inside the fridge door there's a piece of adhesive tape with a warning in German. (The previous owner must have preserved it carefully for decades.) The assassin reads these instructions aloud as if they are a cryptic fragment from ancient times. *Wenn sie parken, stellen Sie ihren caravan immer so, das die Eislade in jeder richtung waagerecht steht.*

'What does it mean?' he asks.

'When parking,' I say, 'always adjust the caravan so the ice shelf is level in both directions.' I think of Anne Carson who took lines from her new microwave user's manual, and ascribed them to the ancient Greek poet Ibykos. Carson calls this technique translation *using the wrong words. A sort of stammering.* I want to share my passion for Anne Carson with the assassin, but he's already winching up one end of the van.

'Check the spirit level!' he shouts.

I watch the bubble wobble at the middle of the neon gauge. 'It's good!' I call back.

The assassin is assiduous. He is the laureate of the spirit level. It's not good enough for him. He winches the van even higher, so that although the bed is flat, the door drops on its hinges. Now the fridge is straight but I have a door that won't close as well as windows that don't lock.

Jack is peering over the gate.

The assassin turns his camouflage-clad back. 'Watch him – he's a thief,' he mutters. 'He's burned out two boats already. Of course, we're on the edges, the fringes here. You'll find it is all shadows and half-truths. This is where crime and dishonesty breed. People steal, deal and set fire to things.'

He looks gravely at me. 'We're an inch beyond the law. The police don't want to come down here, they know not to meddle. If they do have to come, when there's a serious problem, they come in a pack. Most of the enforcement is local. We deal with it ourselves. If you have any trouble, anything at all, tell me – I will make it disappear.'

After he leaves, I take the notepad I lifted from Hôtel JoBo in Paris, and write a to-do list for myself beneath its erotic monogram: *use mallet to level wheels / dig tunnel for hose / buy bin bags / call GP*.

My van is slowly settling on the ground, accepting its level, becoming habitable. I am catching up on long-neglected concerns. In the evening I rattle round, deciding what goes where. I discover the stereo tucked away in a cupboard and play CDs I haven't heard for years. Pergolesi's *Stabat Mater* and a Klaus Nomi selection burned by a friend. The Balkonians, Mike's klezmer band from Berlin. Patti Smith. Bon Iver. The concert continues until the lights and music cut out.

Thursday 10 June

I message the assassin:

> electricity is broken
> please can you help?

come to the shed

Deep in the woods, there's a gingko tree and a stag's horn sumac among the sycamores and oaks, a goji bush growing alongside dewberry and brambles in the undergrowth. I'm intrigued by the rich character of the forest ecology. Behind a screen of bamboo I spot the old shed, with hagstones hanging on strings from the gutters. Here the assassin keeps his tool bench and kettle, but most of the work seems to happen outside. I find him sitting at a rickety picnic table, a pile of clocks in front of him. He winds the hour hands forward as we talk. 'Forgot to do it in the spring,' he says apologetically.

Time may be relaxed here, even malleable, but he probably doesn't want daily interruptions from a new neighbour. I thank him for inviting me over.

'I like sharing useful knowledge.' He extricates a nub of green chalk from a pocket and draws a circuit diagram on the table's wooden slats, beside plans and calculations for other constructions. I recall the equations to calculate watts, amps, voltage from school physics lessons. Would I have paid more attention if the words were written in lichen?

'I like sharing philosophical knowledge too.' He offers me a chocolate biscuit. 'After all, electricity is the new alchemy. Electricity is very deep – sine waves, neutrons and protons and whatnot – but it's also astonishingly simple. As you grapple with the systems in the van, you'll understand this.'

In an equation, problems can be resolved. Balance is restored. For the first time in months, I see myself not as someone who has failed in love and in life but as someone who is learning new skills in order to be able to keep a vehicle off the road.

Diagrams are all very well but the situation requires action. The assassin pads back to the van with me. We examine the control panel above the sink, a row of switches labelled Water Pump, Water Heater, Lights, Fan, Socket. He borrows my eyebrow tweezers to coax fuses out of the tiny boreholes beneath each switch. I would never have guessed the crude plastic casing hid these delicate glass vials with a silver seal at each end.

'Look,' the assassin says. 'People know at what voltage copper and so on will melt, every metal is different. This is how the fuse works, it melts and breaks the circuit when a current becomes unbearably strong. Some appliances take more current, so they need more resilient fuses.'

I squint at the tiny vials. You need keen eyes to see the wire. Some are so slim they're invisible, and the only clue they've blown is a cloud of smoke on the glass.

When I was a child my mother used to encourage me to reach out and touch the electric fences we encountered on our walks: *A shock is good for your heart.* This did teach me resilience. I still expect hardship to be good for me. But sometimes the shock can be too much.

The assassin pulls an electricity meter from his pocket and applies the needles to each end of the car battery, stored under my berth – it beeps. He drops the meter on the draining board and it beeps again: and so I learn that current can be conducted by any surface at all. Any metal that lies in the way. My whole van is a circuit. I am living within a heart-stopping, heart-starting vortex.

'Your battery's fucked,' he concludes. He offers to take it away and recharge it, muttering about sulphides and wet cells. I heave it out of the locker. I've never felt anything so heavy. What a weight it takes to power a home.

Friday 11 June

The morning sun glows through the curtains, dancing across the floor and turning the bedcovers golden. I light the gas under my stovetop kettle and throw Wilkinson's 'Medici' blend in the cafetière.

At the beginning of June 1869 the Scottish naturalist John Muir set out from California's Central Valley into the foothills of the Sierra Nevada with a flock of hundreds of sheep. Muir had been hoping to explore the region, and considered himself fortunate to have found work guiding the animals to their summer pasture. His journals speak of survival on a diet of bread, beans and coffee brewed on a stove.

> Coffee too has its marvels in the camp kitchen but not so many and not so inscrutable as those that beset the bean pot. A low complacent grunt follows a mouthful drawn in with a gurgle and the remark cast forth aimlessly, 'That's

good coffee.' Then another gurgling sip and repetition of the judgement, '*Yes sir*, that *is* good coffee.' As to tea, there are but two kinds, weak and strong, the stronger the better. The only remark heard is, 'That tea's weak,' otherwise it is good enough and not worth mentioning. If it has been boiled an hour or two or smoked on a pitchy fire, no matter, – who cares for a little tannin or creosote? they make the black beverage all the stronger and more attractive to tobacco tanned palates.

Before the windows have even begun to steam up, the gas flame under my kettle peters out. No coffee then. I drink a glass of water and consider where I can find a caffeine fix. And I watch the wren, building a nest of fluff in the crooked branch of a willow.

Wren returns to its nest
and flies out again, in and
out in out all day

I've written a haiku. Old habits must be shifting. Usually I can't write a word before my first cup of coffee, but the wren distracted me, pulled me forward into the day.

I walk down the towpath to Summertown. In the sunshine, this suburb feels like a seaside esplanade. Gingko trees line the Banbury Road. I buy a coffee and an almond pastry from the Lebanese bakery. My galley kitchen is missing bread, butter, honey and cheese – and a saucepan. At Daunts Bookshop, I browse shelves marked INDIA CHINA GERMANY FRANCE ITALY AUSTRALIA MIDDLE EAST.

I spot a new Olivia Laing (essays) and Deborah Levy (*Real Estate*). I mustn't. I must consider the cant of the van, the spirit level and the ice-tray. What am I doing in a bookshop anyway? I was supposed to be going to the Oxfordshire Animal Sanctuary charity shop. Among the bric-a-brac of shot glasses with transfers of Budapest and Coronation mugs I find a set of bright red 1970s Alluflon stackable pots and pans, which fit within one another like matryoshka. Apparently, it's an iconic Italian brand. All seven pans come with a single detachable handle, to be clipped onto whichever one is being used. This means I can use only one pan at a time. No matter.

I've begun writing poems about blots. Blots signify error, spillage, accident, but they are beautiful nonetheless. Some, like those drawn by the Swiss psychologist Hermann Rorschach, can be a leaky fountainhead for new images and ideas. I read about the eighteenth-century artist Alexander Cozens, who as the railways were being laid down across Britain began creating fantastical almost featureless landscapes out of blots. He seems to have developed the idea as a teaching aid, to liberate students whose imagination might be hampered by the (then common) practice of copying the works of the past. Rather than starting out with a blank page, why not start with a blot? *What does it suggest?* he would ask his students. *A tree? A river?* I wonder if the amorphous ink might be read differently now, given concerns about environmental pollution. *What does it suggest? Microscopic plastic beads in the atmosphere? An oil spill seeping over the ocean?* The blots humans make are more often the end of nature.

Cozens describes a true blot as 'forms without lines from which ideas are presented to the mind'. It is a 'production of chance, with a small degree of design'. In this he follows Leonardo da Vinci, who in his *Treatise on Painting* considers how a 'jumble of things: clouds, the ashes from the fire, the mud, or even a pigment-shaped sponge flung against a wall' might 'awaken genius'. I am reminded of Mary Frances, a contemporary artist who takes exquisite photographs of weathered stone, finding wild landscapes through the minute act of close looking at walls and pavements. I think of chance, of taking chances.

My thoughts on happy accidents are interrupted by the arrival of Sven, with a canister of propane hidden under a tarpaulin in his boot. Canisters are in short supply due to Brexit. Wherever did he find it?

'Just some place over in Botley.' I don't press for more information. 'I'll lift it in for you, love. You're not a feminist, are you? I can't stand feminists.'

'Of course I'm a feminist. Aren't you? Give it here.' I lift it into the hold, just big enough for two canisters, at the front of the van – where the old stagecoach driver would sit wrapped in his cloak, if my van were an understudy in a Dickens drama. I grimace.

'See? I can't stand feminists,' says Sven.

'I can't stand misogynists who repeat themselves.'

'Let me look at the leaky window, is it this one?'

'No, it's this one . . .'

'What's wrong with it?' Sven tramples round the van, and pokes at the foam surround. 'Have you got a knife?'

I hand him my Swiss Army knife. He fiddles with the window frame. A bit of the window mechanism, that wasn't broken before, falls off.

'Ah right. That's definitely broken.' He fits it back together again, and smiles at me in satisfaction. Then he notices the real problem, the one I've been trying to tell him about. Meanwhile, I have figured this out – it just requires pressing a button in at the same time as turning a lever. Caravans are a kind of Rubik's Cube of knobs that twist one way or turn the other, doors that open in just the direction they should, so as not to bash into other doors.

'All right, that's fixed. Now let's look at the hot-water tank.'

I'm used to having people in my life who create problems, rather than attempt to solve them. It seems more natural to acclimatise to the problem and deal with the consequences than to figure out a solution. This new approach is making me nervous. Sven pulls the cushions off the berth and opens the locker beneath. He thrusts an arm into the cavity and starts wiggling the tank.

'Are you sure we should move it?' I ask, a bit overwhelmed.

'Yes!' He is exasperated by me, too. 'Where does this cable go?'

He pulls it, and a couple of metres of cable slithers out of the locker. It wasn't plugged in to anything. 'Well, that's another problem cleared up. What a mess.'

'What does this do?' he asks, pointing at the water-heater switch.

'That's the water-heater switch,' I say. 'Did you not read all that stuff I sent you?'

'No. You should never read the instructions. So what happens if we turn it on?'

'Nothing,' I say. 'It's broken.'

He turns it on. Nothing happens.

'It's broken,' he says.

I sense the words I was about to write this afternoon evaporating.

Sven sees me glance at my ancient MacBook. 'You want a PC, love, those things are a complete waste of money.'

'Don't start,' I say. 'I've had this conversation many times with Anna. She worked with virus analysts in Moscow and knew all about this stuff and ...'

'What the hell is *this*?' He points to the charger cable, which hangs onto the plug by a slim metal peg, which sizzles companionably from time to time. 'That's *sparking*. You could set fire to the whole fucking van.'

'I wouldn't,' I say defensively. 'I keep an eye on it.'

'Oh man,' he says. 'What have I got myself into? You're a total nightmare.'

'It's fine. I've been using it for months.'

'Jesus, you're a disaster. That's really dangerous.'

'It doesn't worry me. You just have to make sure it doesn't move once it is plugged in, then it won't spark ...'

'You'll *frazzle*. What use is a frazzled poet? Give me that, what is it? I can pick a new one up on eBay.'

'The plugs are almost as expensive as the laptop. And I'll need a new laptop soon anyway, look the corners are all bashed where I dropped it.'

He starts to remove the hot plug.

'No! I need it to charge the laptop,' I cry. 'I am *working*. Can't you just take a photo of its serial number?'

'I haven't got a camera.'

'Take a photo on your phone.'

'Well, all right, give it here. Oh man, look at this. You could solve it easily enough – it just needs rewiring. Jesus. I'd better get back to base camp. You'll be okay here?'

'Yes,' I plead. 'Please go. Thank you for everything.'

Sven's address is now my *poste restante*. He leaves some parcels. From Kaddy in Cambridge, a writer whose path crossed mine in the Scott Polar Research Institute, an emerald hammock to sling between the willows, and a large bar of soap with the scent of 'Antarctica'. The soap seems too lavish to use in the van's little plastic sink, so I throw it in the chilly overhead locker where I keep my underwear. From Sarah in Bristol, there's an enormous box packed with good things to fill the galley's tiny cupboards: tubes of sundried tomato paste and garlic paste; Chipotle Tabasco Sauce, Green Pepper Tabasco Sauce, a Panang soup base; sachets of dried oregano and paprika and vegetable stock; chilli pepper from Japan; katsu curry sauce and green Thai curry sauce; a sachet of seasoning for pasta puttanesca (Sarah has written on the label, 'This is insanely hot so use sparingly'); precious bars of Rose Otto and Violet Fig chocolate wrapped in greaseproof paper, energy bars as artificial as astronaut food. The box seems bottomless, so I pause and eat a carrot-cake-flavoured energy bar before continuing. Ritter Sport hazelnut chocolate; coffee from the Yirgacheffe wetlands of Ethiopia; Cardhu Gold Reserve Welsh Whisky; breakfast tea; liquorice and peppermint tea; pistachio nuts; cashew nuts; a pack of ready-to-eat refried black beans, Emmental cheese crackers, oatcakes and wheat crackers for cheese; black olives in a salty jar labelled *Olivia d'arancia*, which reminds me of summer evenings in Italy, *Ortiz Bonito del Norte* (tuna) in beautiful red-and-yellow tins; and miniature jars of blackberry-and-apple jam and beetroot chutney with handwritten labels.

There is room for all kinds of rations in a caravan. But your shelves must be well organised.

Saturday 12 June

I wake early, and read in bed before the day begins. Charles Smithson is striding to the Undercliff above Lyme Regis for his fateful encounter with Sarah Woodruff. The dawn woods are like an illuminated manuscript, writes John Fowles, brimful of serene music. One bird stands out, as it does in these woods too: 'A tiny wren perched on top of a bramble not ten feet from him and trilled its violent song. He saw its glittering black eyes, the red and yellow of its song-gaped throat . . . the heart of all life pulsed there in the wren's triumphant throat.'

Sailors once believed that if they carried the feathers of a wren killed on New Year's Day in their pocket, they'd be insured against shipwreck. It's easy to mock others' credulity, but given similar dangers, how would I weigh my life against a wren's? Some superstitions are less cruel. Fear of things to the left is a famous affliction of sailors – never leave or enter a boat using your left foot and if you find a right boot, you'll win good fortune by nailing it to the mast. Sea urchins or 'chalk-eggs' were a remedy used for 'subduing Acrid humours of the stomach' at sea (in other words, seasickness). Anna, mesmerised by the romantic isolation of outer space, told me Yuri Gagarin asked the bus driver taking him to the Baikonur cosmodrome in Kazakhstan to pull over so he could have a piss before walking to the rocket. Thus the last act on land of the first pilot to reach space was to urinate against the rear right-hand tyre of a bus, and all subsequent Russian cosmonauts ceremoniously follow suit. Who wants to enter zero gravity with a full bladder? Closer to home, I have a ritual of dipping the tips of my fingers in the river, and sprinkling a few drops of water on the nape of my neck before launching my kayak. This has practical applications: it is said to prevent cold-water shock. If my van is to be an honorary boat, maybe I should adopt some sailor superstitions. Is the thunderstone enough to keep me safe?

Sunday 13 June

Morning birdsong, and a bike bell *ting*s officiously down the towpath. Some commuter using the canal as a shortcut, bypassing its slow ethos. The lift bridge thuds. I can tell it's a hire boat passing. Tourists play music at high volume to cover up their boredom and shriek in dismay as they approach the low bridge too fast. Everyone on the canal should have a boaters' key that unlocks the lift mechanism (and opens many other secret doors) but not everyone understands its workings. The man who lives in the spick-and-span scarlet boat moored nearest to the bridge is kind and obliging. All hours he emerges to help stricken navigators. Not yet knowing his real name, I call him Sparkles, for everything about him seems polished, even the wheelbarrow he uses to bring food back from the shops. *Alright? Take it easy!* Sparkles shouts reassuringly.

In the distance there's the rumble of lorries, as faint as wind in the trees. I thought it *was* the wind, but the whine of a motorbike picking up speed is unmistakable. I elbow my door open, and peer out. Sunshine. Pink skies lit by flashes of blue from silent yet speeding ambulances. Just visible on the horizon is the overpass on which the ring road crosses the canal and the River Thames.

I walk up the towpath past twelve or so moorings. *Mock Turtle, Battleship Nutmeg, Halcyon, Bramble, Night Hawk, Marmalade Stripe*: many boats are home to families, going by the evidence of cargo bikes and wholesome raised beds of artichokes and chard. Small enclosures are cut into the hedgerows. Some form outdoor dining shelters hung with lanterns, others house dented wheelbarrows and other waterfront ephemera, such as the orange lifebuoy, emblazoned with black letters: DONT PANIC. Do you make your space beautiful or functional? The last mooring is occupied by *Pirate Princess*, a 72-foot bottle-green boat with ranks of solar panels on the roof and planters containing arum lilies, dead dandelions and hydrangeas rather than the usual geraniums and herbs. A skull and crossbones hangs in the window. The regal owner is nowhere to be seen.

The vast concrete stanchions of the overpass are imposing as any of the columns and caryatids on historic buildings in the city centre. Pigeons sun themselves on a ledge, as if re-enacting the famous photo of construction workers eating their sandwiches on a beam over the Manhattan skyline. A motorway sign, which must be several times bigger than my van, directs drivers to 'The Midlands (M40)' with a white arrow on an evergreen background. Most drivers will be unaware of the alternative route just below the fast lane: this waterway, which stretches almost one hundred miles via Banbury and Rugby to join the northern canal network at Coventry. Once a channel for commerce, as the road is now – but already almost obsolete at the time of its building, as industrialists were seduced by the novelty and speed and profit of the railway.

The canal lures me on, but I'll explore another time. As I hurry back to the van, my phone falls on the towpath. The screen shatters. An oily shimmer like the northern lights gleams for a second, then it goes blank. Two years of photographs gone, all my messages. Now I have little connection to the world beyond this community.

In the evening, the hollow call of a cuckoo. Bashō, the seventeenth-century poet and wanderer, writes:

> kankodori
> make lonely
> melancholy me

Woodcutters once listened for the *kankadori* or Himalayan cuckoo when deciding to enter or leave the mountains since its call heralds rain or sunshine, a change in the weather. For Bashō going into the solitude of the mountains or *sabihisha* was a way of connecting with the multitude of existence, as was the call of the bird – its timbre and pitch and volume deepening the receptivity of the human mind.

Monday 14 June

The wren bobs on a branch. There's a glut of willow fluff: on the van roof, on the ground of the glade. John Evelyn, in *Sylva, or A Discourse of Forest-Trees and the Propagation of Timber*, writes:

> A poor body might in an hour's space, gather a pound or two of it, which resembling the finest silk, might doubtless be converted to some profitable use, by an ingenious house-wife, if gather'd in calm evenings, before the wind, rain and dew impair them; I am of opinion, if it were dry'd with care, it might be fit for cushions, and pillows of chastity, for such of old was the reputation of the shade of those trees.

I have another task in mind. I dig a deep hole and fill it with rocks, like an underground alpine grotto, then feed the hosepipe from the bathroom sink into it. Since all the products I'm using are eco-friendly, it's safe to let grey water flow into the ground. The visible network of pipes, these honest systems of water collection and waste disposal are reassuring. They remind me of life in the Arctic, where the ground is often solid rock or permafrost, and such workings cannot be hidden. During the months I spent on Upernavik, my toilet was a plastic bucket lined with a strong yellow sack, which I removed once a week, tied securely, and left in my porch. The waste collector (who surely had pulled the short straw of island employment possibilities) drove the sacks to be incinerated on the other side of the mountain. The arrangement is not so different in the van, except I do the work of disposal myself, lugging the canister of decomposing shit through the forest and down the towpath to the Elsan station, a little brick bothy, where I pour the waste down a chute into the sewage system.

When I came back from Greenland, it took weeks to acclimatise to the gaudy luxury of flushing toilets. The whole bright infrastructure of urban life made me feel uneasy. Its simplicity disguised excess. Now, this step back from society is a necessary act of personal economy, but there's the added benefit of conserving resources.

A blackbird tweaks a worm from the freshly dug earth.

If Jack is a thief, I decide it's in my interests to get to know him better. This requires subterfuge on my part. How do you make friends with a thief?

I decide to ask if he can help me fix my bike lock.

It is rare to board another's boat but Jack invites me for tea on *Bramble* easily and without embarrassment. There's a black-and-white chart of the Newfoundland coast on the wall by the hatch, and a mahogany barometer beneath it. The fridge is full of bottles of alcohol-free beer, and there are more bottles in the sink.

'I would never have a dishwasher,' Jack says as he rinses out the teapot, ignoring his cellar arrangements. 'Have you read Kahlil Gibran's *The Prophet*? Great book. "Comfort is the death of the soul."'

Out the window I watch a squirrel empty one of his bird feeders. Interesting to see the towpath from a boater's perspective. The window on the other side looks onto the marshes where rhododendrons and flag irises are in flower. Jack talks slowly and deliberately: he has a weak heart, he tells me, so in winter he can't go out till the thermometer rises to zero degrees or the cold will thicken his blood. He must be especially careful in the woods; he has learned to avoid the shadows cast by trees.

He bends over the locking mechanism, as if it's a ouija board. Greasy hair tied back with a blue elastic band. Beads of sweat on his brow. He complains he was woken by sirens on the overpass last night. He hasn't slept at all. Now Sparkles' whistling is the only sound that disturbs the peace. The clunk of the bridge as someone crosses the canal.

'What do you think?' I ask as he tinkers.

'I think it will give me a coronary,' says Jack morosely, 'and that would be a blessing.'

But he sees the solution. Not only that, turns out he can dowse for spirits too. He describes the chill of a presence down his back, like cold hands gripping his shoulders and shaking him.

'If your van is ever haunted, I can help you,' he says.

'Thanks,' I say. The visit is not going quite as I expected.

He hands the lock back with a laugh. 'You can pay me in poems. Heuch! Heuch!'

Tuesday 15 June

*Oxford is – Oxford. Perhaps it wants its inmates to love it
rather than to love one another.*
E. M. Forster, *Howards End*

During my three years of study at Oxford I didn't spend long in university halls. I found my thoughts drowned out by more assertive voices, so I took off on National Express bus journeys, relishing my reading list but also the freedom to look beyond it and discover distractions on the road. I spent precious hours that ought to have been dedicated to research in the library seeking out alternative Oxfords. I tramped through overgrown cemeteries where spies were rumoured to have left drops during the Cold War and I made a pilgrimage to the source of the Thames. I walked along the canal, yearning to live on a narrowboat and little thinking one day I'd spurn one in favour of a van. (How could I have known, crossing my future path, that I would come to know the sound of this bridge so well, that I was passing a boat on which friends would live?) University regulations forbade students having a job, but I couldn't have survived without an income, so I put in weekend shifts at the Hi-Lo restaurant on the Cowley Road, coming back to college at dawn with boxes of leftover jerk chicken to sustain me through the week. Later, I sold groceries to my professors disguised in a blue staff tabard in the Jericho Co-Op. I came to know the customers who hid cheese and cold meats under their coats because they couldn't afford food. Merely ignoring them as they shuffled out of the door seemed a passive way to help, so I began to volunteer in the night shelter in Speedwell Street, ladling baked beans over margarine-slick potatoes and listening to people's stories.

For years I worried that I'd flunked my golden opportunity to study, since others considered these activities merely displacement. Yet it seems that I was actually honing a working method: I instinctively treated Oxford as the first in many attempts to understand a place. My reading list was the distraction, the road my real study.

Now I am landing back here again, as unexpected as a rock from space, a stunned meteorite. It may be that the force of my falling will slam me deeper than ever into the earth.

I walk into the city. Rats bounce across the towpath ahead of me, hiding in the alder clumps that braid the bank. The alder's timbers, according to Evelyn, were frequently sought after 'for such buildings as lie continually under water, where it will harden like a very stone'. He writes that 'they us'd it under that famous Bridge at Venice, the *Rialto*, which passes over the *Gran-Canal*, bearing a vast weight'. Trees do petrify due to mineralisation, but Evelyn knew only that the process could not be hurried – 'in tract of time, it turns to stone; which perhaps it may seem to be (as well as other aquatick) where it meets with some lapidescant quality in the earth and water'.

The narrowboats moored opposite the private school's sports field are painted neat complementary colours: sky blue and indigo, maroon and sage green. *Portsea* looks like a museum exhibit, with its traditional diamond paintwork, brass trumpet horn and ropes neatly coiled on the roof. All narrowboats declare the yard or waterway they hail from, and *Portsea*'s plaque identifies its origin as a wharf in Camden Town. As well as permanent residents and visiting cruisers, there are hire boats named after university colleges: *Keble*, *Magdalen*, *Queens*. This stretch of the canal is home to the most sinister boat I have seen on any waters: a gunboat-grey vessel without a name that has been here for over twenty years. I have made many journeys since my first sighting of it, and I wonder about the owner's spell on this mooring in the meantime. Some say Pierre took one too many trips and never came down. He claims to be the Earl of Swansea, and the only British samurai. Six or seven feral cats flinch as I approach and run from me to hide under the wonky solar panels and assorted things that may come in useful one day, piled on the roof: broken chair legs, antique wine crates, lifebuoys, old tin cans. The iron tang of meat hangs in the air.

By the Elizabeth Jennings Way bridge, a man in a panama hat is playing a loutar. Here, the city begins. Grand terraces back onto the canal, with smooth lawns on which ducks are dozing. The wild dog rose is upstaged by rambling roses that tumble over garden trellises and gazebos dressed with fancy ironwork furniture. The bridge is named after a writer who haunted Oxford from her time here as a student, and for a while held down a job in the city's Central Library. Poetry was Elizabeth Jennings' 'temporary home', her 'fulcrum' in a peripatetic life. She wore a duffle coat to be honoured by the Queen for her contribution to British Poetry at Buckingham Palace, a style that now seems ahead of the trend. But this once-beloved writer has fallen out of fashion since her death in 2001. Unkindly called 'the bag lady of the sonnets', and even described as 'ramshackle' by her biographer Dana Greene, that reputation rests on an all-too-common story: a good landlord dies, the tenant is evicted by a new unscrupulous landlord, and searches for permanent residence while drifting between temporary addresses. Greene quotes the unpublished poem 'On the Move Again', in which Jennings writes that she considered herself 'a parcel', sent to and fro, stamped with 'not known here'. She posted notices around town: 'Elizabeth Jennings has nowhere to live. Can you help?' I warm to the tone of sardonic humour in her shameless appeal, knowing all too well the desperation it may have masked.

There are still traces of Jennings in the city, and I often feel her presence in Jericho, where she would visit the cinema in the afternoons and work on translations of Michelangelo's sonnets in cafes late into the evenings, lingering over a glass of wine until she could no longer delay going back to her lodgings. There are living ghosts here too, people whose stories I know (or guess) without knowing the people, really, or them knowing me. Characters whose paths cross mine over and over, like the septuagenarian heavy metal giant wearing skinny black jeans, with silver skull rings on his fingers. The tall man sporting state-of-the-art headphones, shambling down the towpath after his golden retriever, is a respected humanitarian and former BBC foreign correspondent, whose chisel face once stared from the screen to a background of missiles over Belgrade and Baghdad. We give each other the hint of a smile. The parent teaching her children the names of the trees beside the Thames is the city's Labour MP, and currently the Shadow Chancellor – one of the brilliant spirits of a dull and corrupt House.

The canal comes to an end – or begins – only a few streets from the Bodleian Library, where the water slips under a rusty bridge at Sheepwash Lock, and into a stagnant basin.

Many shops have closed and from their gutted interiors Covid testing centres have sprung. I take my phone to Javed at Only Connect on the Cornmarket for repair. He also deals in vape supplies and tourist merchandise. Rows of plastic Elvises rotate their hips gently, a shelf of Queen Elizabeth IIs sway and wave their white-gloved hands. While Javed melts the back off my phone, I browse the vape flavours: blackcurrant, mint, strawberry, pure.

A tourist from Birmingham drifts in: 'Do you have any tea towels?'

Javed waves dismissively to the Harry & Meghan Wedding Commemorative items beside the till.

'Is that all?' she says.

'Yes,' he says. 'No one buys tea towels now.'

My phone will be an overnight job. Javed takes my number. I explain that it belongs to the phone I am leaving with him, the one that doesn't ring any more. He shrugs and follows me out, and begins putting transparent umbrellas with Mickey Mouse ears over the racks of postcards, with their misty views of the Sheldonian Theatre and the Bridge of Sighs. It is raining again. 'No one buys postcards now,' he tells me.

Examinations are finishing. Pavements are spangled with glitter, chalk dust, cosmic confetti – pink green yellow – and shaving foam where students have bombed each other. Champagne corks in the gutters. In the supermarket, carnations wilt in buckets by the checkout, no longer required for the buttonholes of student gowns.

I walk back through the woods with a plastic-wrapped bouquet – the salvaged yellow flowers look cheerful arranged on the windowsill in a yoghurt pot.

Wednesday 16 June

After a fortnight, I invite Anna to the van for tea. It's an ambitious expedition: two bus journeys across town, then the lane with its potholes. But circumstances prevent her making it all the way.

She stands forlorn on the verge as the bus pulls away, and tells me she has to go back home immediately. She's just had a call from her sister with bad news: Serge, their father, has been diagnosed with leukaemia. A terminal prognosis: four months. We cross to the stop on the opposite side of the road, where the glass has shattered and left an empty metal frame, and I wait with her until the bus returns. I kiss her cheek through the mask: goodbye.

The mundane effort of Anna's wasted journey magnifies my sorrow at her news. I wish I could have given her a cup of tea at least. I walk back to the van alone, brooding on Serge and his daughter. Anna is still vulnerable and although she seldom saw her father during lockdown, his illness affects the equilibrium of her small support network. For the second time since her stroke, I'm aware that I could choose either to disappear or to take responsibility for both our stories in the months ahead. This time, something has shifted. I still fear the latter choice may ravage my own brittle resources and twist an erratic existence out of all recognisable shape. But I also value the unconventional friendship we are tentatively forging, and I'm curious to see where the metamorphosis leads. 'One mourns when one accepts that by the loss one undergoes one will be changed, possibly forever,' writes the philosopher Judith Butler. 'Perhaps mourning has to do with agreeing to undergo a transformation (perhaps one should say submitting to a transformation) the full result of which we cannot know in advance. There is losing, as we know, but there is also the transformative effect of loss.'

I pick young bright leaves for beech-leaf noyau, a drink that originated nearby in the Chilterns, where beech woods were husbanded in the eighteenth and nineteenth centuries for the chair-making trade. I pack the leaves in an old bottle and pour gin over them, then hide it under the berth to steep for a few weeks.

Thursday 17 June

The Cherwell Valley line is the main route towards Birmingham and connections on to the north and Scotland. I used to travel it often. I would be on those CrossCountry trains. Looking out of the window as we drew into Oxford, curious about the scrubby dwellings I glimpsed through the trees. I remember the lull of movement, the carton of tea in its hollow on the seat tray, the filmic unspooling of landscape. Now the carriages flash past the caravan, almost empty of passengers. The sound of the trains is an assurance that other places still exist. At the beginning of lockdown, the prospect of borders closing caused me a wild despair. Readings around the UK and in Europe were cancelled, tentatively rescheduled and cancelled again. Now the despair has been replaced by a dull ache. I used to see travel as the graft, the hardship I pressed my weight against to find shelter, or the shape of a story. The ordeal now is learning to stay in place, endurance. If I wait until my bones ache with the effort of stillness, what will come to me?

Sven drives over, with this week's gift: a new plug for my adaptor. It was free, he says. No more fried poets. I'm surprised how having support with these small problems makes bigger things – like life – seem possible. He also brings spare ribs for the assassin and a chicken carcass for the dogs.

'Caravan not floated away yet?' He looks at my ankles. 'I see the mozzies can't get enough of you.'

'I have my medicine.' I wave a tube of ointment at him.

'You don't need medicine,' Sven says. 'You need a killing machine.'

We wander through the woods, and are greeted by a shout from inside the shed: 'WHO THE FUCK IS ON MY LAND?'

When the assassin sees us, he replaces his rifle behind the door and pulls out deckchairs from under a tarp. 'This is a Social Occasion,' he announces. The deckchairs are the old-fashioned kind with striped canvas seats and sprung legs. Spiders leap out when I open them up.

'Would you like a couple for the van? I've got plenty,' he offers. He found them at the house-clearance shop on Windmill Road.

'Jesus, you don't want that crap knocking around,' says Sven.

The assassin looks hurt. 'Not everyone lives in suburbia with widescreen TV and John Lewis sun-loungers.'

'These are great.' I stroke the rusting armrests. 'Thanks, I'll take a few.'

The assassin is writing an advert for the paper. He shows it to me. 'If you have a lot of adjectives, you want to put commas between them, right?'

'Yes, generally,' I say.

'If there's a *big beautiful boat* you'll put a comma between *big* and *beautiful*, but not after *beautiful*?'

'Yes.'

'But the people writing adverts don't put any commas in at all.'

'Adverts are different,' says Sven. He tells an Arabic proverb about a man who opened a fish shop. 'He puts a sign up over the door: هنا يُباع السمك. *Fish sold here.* A customer came and said to him, "Why put the word *here*? Aren't fish sold in other places?" So he deleted the word *here*. Another customer said, "There's no need for the word *sold*, it's obvious you're not giving it away." So he deleted the word *sold*. Then a third came and said, "There's no need to advertise the fish, since people can see and smell it." So he took down the sign.'

'And the Oxford comma,' says the assassin, ignoring him. 'It's always been controversial, hasn't it. Everyone wants you to take it out. No one knows the basics any more. No one knows where the commas go.'

'A comma is a pause, a breath,' I say. 'Gertrude Stein didn't use commas, she wanted her readers to decide for themselves when to take a breath. She believed commas were servile.'

'Really?' says the assassin. If his interest is feigned it is convincing. 'Well, detail is important. How about saying *beautiful big boat*? Writing's like martial arts. You need the groundwork, and then you can flow.' He kicks Sven playfully on the butt.

Sven kicks back. 'What'll the line-up be tonight then? Four four two?' England is in the semi-final. He knows the assassin does not care.

Friday 18 June

I sit in my new, old deckchair, drinking coffee and reading Anna Tsing's *The Mushroom at the End of the World*. A book about foraging, and forest lives. 'Global landscapes today are strewn with ruin,' Tsing writes, yet she believes 'places can be lively despite announcement of their death.' The first living thing to emerge from the blasted landscape around Hiroshima after the atom bomb was a matsutake mushroom. The prized matsutake – 'the most valued mushroom on earth', given as a gourmet gift in Japan – is a resilient renegade. It cannot be cultivated, and grows in wild and unexpected places. Tsing describes mushroom hunts deep in the Cascade Mountains in the US: Asian immigrants and refugees from the Mien, Hmong, Lao and Khmer communities gather, many equipped with jungle skills from the Indochinese wars. Harvesting matsutake becomes a salve for war trauma as well as a means of earning a livelihood.

The cuckoo calls. *In May, I sing night and day. In June I change my tune.*

A green amphitheatre surrounds me – the nettle leaves are too tough this late in the year for soup and risotto, but the seeds hanging in threads from the female flowers are rich in vitamins and, being a stimulant, they make a good tea. Some people even consider them an acceptable substitute for coffee. An inch from the van's front wheel, there's a small gooseberry bush. If we'd pushed a fraction further, it would have been crushed.

Six hawthorn trees in pots have appeared at the gate overnight. Hawthorn is the new currency of the canal. Everyone deals in them: mysterious drops, the secret code of saplings.

A woman pushing a huge golden chrysanthemum in a wheelbarrow stops, and adds the hawthorns to her load. I've seen Aislin in passing a couple of times but she's been on a different trajectory, like a fast-moving centrifuge whose still centre rests in these woods. Now she loads the saplings into her barrow and comes up the path. She's light on her feet, light of smile.

'You need a bell for the gate, don't you?' she says. 'So you have warning of visitors. We'll dig one out for you.' She asks if I'll look after the hens while they go away for the weekend.

I'd love to. I tell her about the unexpected gooseberry.

'There's a wild raspberry in the woods – you could take a cutting,' says Aislin. 'I want to start a vegetable patch near the bee-hives, too.' The soil is rich here, good for vegetables. Wildflowers prefer poor soil. Like some people, they need to be put in a hard place to thrive. She gives me a keen stare, and tells me about the forest tradition in Theravāda Buddhism, begun by Ajahn Mun, who was ordained as a monk in 1893. Mun wandered the forests of Thailand, Burma and Laos, looking for secluded places where he would spend hours in meditation. He developed thirteen *dhuthanga* or ascetic practices, rules for simple living by eating alms and wearing clothes made from cast-off rags. Five of the *dhuthanga* relate to places of residence. Aislin recites them: to dwell in a forest away from village distractions; to dwell beneath a tree's branches; to dwell on the bare earth without even a tree for shelter; to be content to dwell by the graveyard gates; and finally, the 'any-bed-user's practice' or *yatha-santhatik'anga*, to be satisfied with any dwelling you are given.

'You're a nun,' she says with a smile. 'A Buddhist nun visited us once . . . we had a caravan for guests then, and so we set up the sofa for her as a bed, like you have, but she slept on the floor – the cushions were too soft for her, she said.'

'I'm more of an anchorite than nun,' I say. 'Like Julian of Norwich. Looking for visions.'

'Maybe you're our hermit? Every wood needs a hermit.' She lifts the wheelbarrow. 'I want to finish the hedge before we set off.'

'Would you like a hand?'

Anna taught me to love new foods. Georgian walnut and coriander dips and sweet fizzy red wines, borscht, shakshuka, sauces made with black and orange tomatoes from our own growbag vines, mushroom dumplings, all sorts of delicious surprises wrapped in tiny pastry parcels, sour soups with stale white bread. One of the first dishes she made for me was the complex and colourful dressed salad known as 'herring under a fur coat'. Herring every which way. I loved these foods first because I loved her, and in the end I loved their astringent taste for its own sake.

After planting a hedge twenty hawthorns long, I boil some new potatoes Aislin has given me, and add dill, capers and finely chopped spring onion, an emulsion of white wine vinegar, olive oil. The sharp smell of vinegar and herbs fills the van and I realise that I am crying as I slice the steaming potatoes to soak up the oils. It's a relatively small regret, not to be able to share this meal with Anna; there are greater concerns in both our lives. We message almost every evening, now she can use speech-to-text software on her phone. But the pain caused by the emptiness of this activity without her is enormous. At the same time, I'm relieved no longer to have to endure the tension of those sad, silent lockdown meals. Our lives together had become so entangled with despair that it effected a kind of paralysis in both of us. I realise now how much I loved her, despite my fury at her slow, mysterious diminishment. This is a strange grief, for someone who is lost, but not lost, someone no more than ten miles away, someone I can send a message to, to say I am thinking of her, of the many meals we have shared (the whole caravan smells of dill, should I add a chopped boiled egg?). How do you mourn such a nuanced loss? How to acknowledge the grief at the same time as celebrating Anna's miraculous survival, her new mode of being?

I curse the fickle luxury of health. In China Miéville's story *Perdido Street Station*, Yaghagarek, a member of the hawk race, is de-winged for his crime of 'choice theft'. Illness is one of the 'choice thefts', an action that denies another being the right to choose their own fate.

The thought of Yaghagarek reminds me that I must see to the chickens before dusk falls, for fox cubs are weaned in June; they have abandoned their dens, and are hungry. Aislin and the assassin live behind a system of gates, each one with a baffling locking mechanism forged in the workshop. Cowbells hang from wire twine and make a symphony of clonks as I progress through the maze. There is a small bell on the door of the chicken coop too. Back in their run, the hens scratch hopefully at the tired soil, casting their claws out behind them. I am soothed by the bells, and the mournful crooning of the chickens as I scatter corn in their trough and shut them safely in.

Saturday 19 June

This morning, I retrace my steps through the maze and open the back of the henhouse and reach inside. Two warm eggs in the hay. I take them, and replace them with the ghost eggs Aislin showed me yesterday.

She opened a drawer in the workshop, and four ceramic ovals rolled towards us. A hole at each end, as if blown. There was not a smudge on them but I could tell they were old. I was reminded of the blackbird funnel you place in a pie dish, with its beak pointing skywards, in which the steam becomes its song.

'Dusty is broody,' Aislin said. 'If you take away her eggs, she'll not like it. She makes a new nest somewhere else. She goes to great lengths to stop anyone taking her eggs. It's very trying to keep hunting for a new nest every few days. So every morning when you take an egg from the roost, you roll one of these eggs into it. She never notices the difference.'

Thanks to this porcelain proxy the ancient ritual of egg theft can continue. But what if the hen knows the trick all along? What if she has her own reasons to be content to warm beneath her feathers this cold and hollow shell.

It rains all day. Sven comes in the evening, bringing a silver tarpaulin, which looks suspiciously new, to cover my bike.

'Just had it lying around,' he says.

'You can't keep buying me things,' I say.

'But you're my pet poet,' he says. 'My very own Dylan Thomas.'

'I'm not your pet,' I say, petulantly. I consider the tarpaulin and other tools he has brought for the van. His open door and his endless advice. How he lets me use his address for post. Maybe the van is his pet?

Older relatives once called me pet. But all of them were female. I think of petting.

'Please don't call me your pet.'

'All right, pet.'

Since he will not be persuaded, I turn the problem on its head and consider him a patron. Dylan Thomas is an example of how not to do it. For a while, Dylan and Caitlin lived a few miles downriver in the grounds of Magdalen College. Margaret Taylor, the wife of modern history don A. J. P. Taylor, had invited the couple to move into their summerhouse in 1946. Some versions of the story say they came for dinner, and could not be persuaded to leave. As Margaret's infatuation with Dylan grew, so did the don's despair. Thomas and Taylor had little in common apart from a liking for literature and beer. Taylor was making a conscientious attempt at wartime rationing, but his summerhouse guest drank the house beer barrel dry. By 1947, the arrangement was not practicable any longer, and Margaret was forced to find Caitlin and Dylan a manor nearby, where they lived for two years. Later she bought them the Boat House, a safe distance away on the Welsh coast at Laugharne. The Taylors separated in 1950.

Lightly beating the fresh eggs for spaghetti carbonara, I tell Sven I'm concerned about Anna. He says that I have to reconsider my loyalty to her.

'It feels so selfish to walk away like this,' I say.

'No. It's like any kind of rescue, imagine if you were out on the water. You know the rules on the river: you have to save yourself first. Save yourself from the weir. Then worry about the other person. Or, even better, call someone else to help the other person. I mean, you're not any use anyway in the state you're in, are you?'

'No.' My voice is muffled.

'No,' he says. 'Quite right. You're a wreck.'

I let the word *wreck* settle. I hadn't viewed myself as broken, just exhausted. Lines from the Adrienne Rich poem 'Diving into the Wreck' drift into my head and out again. I pour chilled Picpoul de Pinet into a couple of jam jars.

'You can't just walk into a caring role unsupported yourself, like you did. It's hardcore. Look at what I do for my mam. There are guys, they've served in Afghanistan, they've shot the Taliban, they faced death on a daily basis, but they'll never put their mam in a hoist or wipe her private parts when she's shat herself. They just can't deal with it. They don't know the half of what bravery is.'

A dogfight erupts on the towpath. Low snarls, a yelp, more snarls.

'You have to let go,' he says. 'Anna has to get on with her life. You have to get on with yours. Now, what else needs sorting?'

'Well, the van battery keeps running down . . .'

A train approaches and the reverberations tremble up through the ground. The caravan rocks in its airstream, and spaghetti unfurls from Sven's fork. I have begun to distinguish different operators by sound and speed. As E. M. Forster writes in *Howards End*: 'The low rich purr of a Great Western express is not the worst background for conversation.' Sven imagines carriages coming off the track in the night, he says, and careening into the van. It sounds like a Buster Keaton movie. 'You'd be toast!' he says, with relish.

Later, as I'm falling asleep, I listen to the trains pass, making a banshee scream or a sound like a bullet that pierces the van. Sometimes in the hush that follows I catch another sound, a faint electronic sigh, as the points change. The trains make the wildness. Without the occasional scream and the shaking, I would not appreciate the silence and stillness. How fast they travel and how brutal their force. My heart tenses, as I realise how easily I could climb the barrier and lay myself down on the rails. How impossible to move out of the way in time, if you changed your mind.

Sunday 20 June

I am woken by the chiffchaff. Its unvaried song relentless, the shrill double note without nuance.

The common is blazing with buttercups and vetches, soft silvery grasses and sweet clover. Pollen thick as smoke in the warm air. A herd of cattle grazes the hazy expanse from railway to road and back again, and two piebald ponies dip their muzzles in the river skirting its western edge. Three hundred years ago and more, this pasture was used for horse racing, and low stone bridges laid over washes and ditches hint at the former course. Sailing skiffs tack up and down from the boat club. This is an old land, where the Thames still flows undercover using the name Isis, an arcane suffix from Latin *Tamesis* and proto-Celtic *Tamēssa*, possibly meaning 'dark'.

My ancestors were people whose lives and livelihoods depended on close looking at and through sights: weavers and soldiers, farmers and saddlers. When my father left school, he had to follow his father to agricultural college, before he was allowed to fulfil his dream of studying sculpture. I wonder how it was to go from the timeless rituals of the fields to the fugitive fashions of 1960s Soho. He did not disown his agricultural past. The greatest wonder of his study to me as a child was not the bronze busts of composers and politicians but a wooden cabinet filled with dusty jars containing the grass seed heads he'd collected at college. He'd lavished his creative instincts on the project, making a display as elegant as any of Joseph Cornell's boxes. Each jar contained a single specimen, with a handwritten label: Timothy, Crested Dog's-tail, Cock's-foot, Yorkshire Fog and Bentgrass. Also Meadow Foxtail. Italian Ryegrass and Perennial Ryegrass, too, and the fescues: Sheep's Fescue, Tall

Fescue, Red Fescue and Meadow Fescue. Those jars were a lesson in the importance of detail; they showed me that a field that appears green or yellow from a distance is a medley of colours and species when you lie down in the grass and look close.

I meet Prerona on the way to her allotment. She is tireless, tending to her own plot after a day of doing other people's gardens. 'You should never look at a gardener's allotment,' she tells me. Like writers' notebooks. Everyone needs a secret space in which to mess up.

Prerona gives me a cutting of catmint. White roots forged in water, destined for the dark earth.

The allotments are an unexpected square of tillage in the middle of the common. According to legend the common itself has never been ploughed. By the gates are two ancient hawthorns. They remind me of a story in the *Metamorphoses*, about Baucis and Philemon, an old couple who were turned into trees. Ovid tells how Zeus and Hermes were travelling, disguised as ordinary mortals, and like ordinary mortals, they could find nowhere to rest and quench their thirst. Every door remained closed to them. Only Baucis and Philemon welcomed the two strangers, unaware they were serving gods until they noticed that the beech-wood cups were never without wine. Their neighbours were cursed for their ignorance and tightfistedness – but the old couple, when their time came to die, were turned to trees.

A pair of lost spectacles are hanging in one of the hawthorns, and in the other perches a crow with a grey head. It watches me follow a desire track down to the Thames, which sweeps in wide oxbow bends towards the city. A lone fisherman is standing under the willows. He's weighed down with an assortment of nets and rods, like a busker, a one-man band about to start drumming a watery beat on his large round net. But fishermen are always silent.

Monday 21 June

Solstice. I dream there are silver keys and coins buried in the dark earth beneath the van.

Tuesday 22 June

Aislin brings a gift: pelargoniums, their fluted leaves dusky with the scent of Old Spice and cinnamon. As if the eggs were not enough reward for feeding the chickens.

Two trains shudder past at once, heading in different directions. In the early days of the railway, Aislin says, collisions were much more frequent than they are now. In the 1860s, a doctor called Erichsen noticed that some survivors reported symptoms – confusion, hearing voices, and paralysis – although they didn't seem to be injured. He called this phenomenon 'railway spine'. Erichsen's findings led Sigmund Freud to develop his ideas on memory and trauma. The failings of the railway revealed that the mind could be wounded as much as the body.

We practise t'ai chi together by the bamboo. Single whip. Waving arms like clouds. Jade girl shoots shuttle. Be in this moment. Now be in this moment. She halts her slow form to move a snail off the path, and we step weightless on the shining trail it leaves behind.

A freight train passes on its way southwards to Port of Southampton from the Midlands. The containers ease to a halt where the points meet, and there's silence for a second. Then the groan of a break being lifted, and wheels grind on along the rails. The heavy colours of old industry flicker past. Names that evoke ancient, distant seas: Chronos, 'k' line, Triton, Alia, Magellan. Anonymous, huge blue containers. Some carriages bear no load, so that sunlight glimmers in the gap – and the whole train becomes a score: empty space, empty space, empty space, empty space, empty space, empty space, Tex, Triton, huge blue, huge blue.

When the venerable t'ai chi master Chen Bing travelled from his village in China to New York to teach, he was given a studio under the viaduct of the El train. His students complained that the noise of the trains was making it impossible for them to concentrate. 'Those are not trains,' Chen Bing said. 'They are dragons.'

Dragons continue to circuit the world, even when people cannot travel. The freight trains form a chain that keeps commerce moving: Hong Kong, Hamburg, Trieste. Oxford. But what is inside the containers?

The van is no bigger than these speedier cousins, which travel in a true 'caravan', forty or so at a time. Often the grey containers of the Danish firm Maersk, the world's biggest shipping company. While I was in Denmark looking for thunderstones, the patriarch of Maersk died and was given a state funeral. Mærsk Møller's last journey made the evening news: the polished hearse conveying its precious goods to the Copenhagen chapel; the loyal assistant in tears; a glimpse of royalty. The newsreel cut from the hearse to footage of more containers, each branded with a white star on a blue square, a legacy that continues to circle the seas.

The rusting carriages on which the containers ride are each branded too – with an image of a sailing boat. The freight trains have an identity as complex as my road-going Buccaneer, with its logo of a tall ship, pennants swirling in the salt breeze. If our vehicles could speak to each other in that moment of passing (*'alright?'*), what tales they'd tell of their adventures.

Wednesday 23 June

The first trees were ferns. They are primal. Charcoal and oil are made out of ferns that existed at the beginning of life. There are many stories and folktales about plants having memories [and] ferns may contain secret knowledge.
Anselm Kiefer

Elderflower heads are turning brittle and brown. I gather a last batch for cordial and save some of the florets for a posy. A sprig of fennel goes in the jar too, and a few blowsy opium poppies. Derek Jarman loved the 'mauve nostalgia' of these flowers.

In the evening I walk to the village and settle into the corner table in Jacob's Inn, which is becoming my regular spot when I wish to escape the hazards of the van. The waiter greets me as if I am his oldest friend. I dive into my neglected inbox. I dread what I might find, but there are good things. Sarah Thomas, who sent the yarrow during lockdown, asks for an endorsement for her book, *The Raven's Nest*. Later, walking home past illuminated boat windows, I call Sarah and apologise for my delayed response, explaining my difficulty accessing email. She tells me tonight is Jónsmessunótt, when seals shed their slippery skins and take the guise of women.

Midsummer Eve: a night when those of us who are not seals in disguise should turn our clothes inside out to protect ourselves from enchantment, and carry rue in our pockets. Light bonfires and scatter the ashes on our crops at dawn. Collect spores from the underside of fern leaves. At a time of light, honour the plants that grow in the shade. The artist Anselm Kiefer wrote: 'Ferns remind us that we also need the darkness.' In his series *Johannisnacht*, Kiefer collaged ferns onto lead pigment, and the plants' dried bracts appear also, alongside brambles and mistletoe, against a background of cracked and desiccated clay in his installation *Secrets of the Ferns*. A new herbarium, an archive of the vanished past for a disappearing future.

Ferns were not the first plants on the planet – mosses, hornworts, and liverworts have clung to the ground for 500 million years. Ferns appeared a hundred million years or so later, in the middle Devonian period. In the Carboniferous they began their slow transmutation into the fossil fuels that powered the Industrial Revolution, and much human motion since. Fern species prevailed as the dinosaurs fell, through extinction after extinction, enduring glaciations and volcanic eruptions; those that survive today are living fossils.

The reproduction of ferns was considered so unfathomable that Carl Linnaeus, the Swedish naturalist, classified them using the term *Cryptogamia* ('hidden marriage'). Folk believed that at dusk on Midsummer's Eve, a tiny blue flower bloomed on the bracken, in which an invisible seed ripened. This seed could be collected on a stack of twelve pewter plates – it would fall through the first eleven plates and scatter on the last at midnight. The fortunate few who succeeded in collecting these seeds were said to have achieved invisibility, but presumably they had disappeared by other means. Only with the discovery of 'fern dust' by John Lindsay, a surgeon and botanist working in Jamaica in the 1780s, did humans begin to understand the action of spores.

Ferns achieved cult status in the Victorian era, when the railways created new routes to Britain's wild, damp corners. (With a neat synergy, the coal that powered the steam trains carrying collectors was composed of the ferns' Carboniferous ancestors.) Fern fever or 'pteridomania' was also aided by the invention in 1829 of the Wardian case, a glass box like Sleeping Beauty's coffin built to convey the sensitive plants back to the cities. This elegant mode of transport soon became a method of display. Some ferns never escaped these cases, which – once sealed – became terrariums, the forerunners of today's bottle gardens.

A late train speeds north and its lights sweep past the van's foggy windows in a molten stream. Branches sway and are still. A huge yellow moon is rising, fast, over the rails. I remember watching the moon from the gilded balcony on my last night in the Künstlerhaus. I couldn't have imagined any of this then: the upheaval I'm living with until I get the water heater working, or the pleasure it gives me to boil a kettle to wash in, or the work I've done against the odds, words written between attempting to resolve the van's muddles and my own. I draw the curtains and work until after midnight, stopping only for a supper of sardines on toast (burned) washed down with today's infusion of elderflower. At last I blow the candles out, and the smoke sets off the fire detector. I flap the windows back and forth until the beeps subside.

A mob of crows clatters up from the woods in alarm.

Thursday 24 June

Midsummer. Serge has been admitted to a hospice.

It's cold, my boots are soggy. I fill the Aquaroll. Prerona has left a pot of parsley beneath the standpipe to catch the drips. Hosepipe in hand, I stare into space. I think of all the things I never said to Serge. Tiny white flowers are emerging among the bramble thorns – I'll suggest to Anna that we make jam together this autumn.

I trundle back to the van past Jack's boat. 'Alright?' he says. I nod, and scurry on. I'm not feeling alright at all.

There's an iron taste in my mouth. In order to displace the pain I feel for Serge, for Anna, I spend an hour digging, forcing energy into the earth with the spade's blunt blade, until my back aches and my legs tremble with fatigue. Aislin says the thighs are known as 'little hearts' in Chinese medicine, because they too have chambers or valves to pump blood around the body. My own heart seems to have swollen until it occupies my whole chest. Sometimes, these days, I can barely breathe. The organ feels awry. Has my heart turned cannibal? Is it eating me? I thump my chest, hard, many times, trying to silence the inner pain with an outer pain of my own making.

The nettles are already rebounding from my pass with the assassin's scythe. Farmers know this as the *aftermowth*, the second crop that grows after the first has been mown or harvested, from which the term 'aftermath' derives. The nettles' dense canopy has long prevented other plants growing, and I want the aftermath to be different. I plant a bronze fennel at the corner of the van, where it will catch the sun. In the shade, each side of the van door, a bushy, exuberant Ursula's Red fern, and in the freshly dug soil, deer ferns and a common polypody. I hope the ferns will bring their secret knowledge of deep time, their watery strength and mystical trans-formation, to the glade. Croziers will unfurl from the furred corms.

Pinnate fronds will split the sunlight. Spores will darken and swell. Soon the view from my study will be even greener than that of the greenest reading room I know, the Lyrik Kabinett in Munich where two years ago I sat looking onto walls of ivy and moss, and reading *Nox*, Anne Carson's book about the suicide of her brother. A riff on Catullus' elegy for his own brother. She writes, 'Nothing in English can capture the passionate, slow surface of a Roman elegy . . . Catullan diction, which at its most sorrowful has an air of deep festivity, like one of those trees that turns all its leaves over, silver, in the wind . . . I guess it never ends. A brother never ends.' Surrounded by silver leaves, I wonder how sorrow and festivity might be written, or even sung. Orpheus carried willow branches on his pilgrimage to the Underworld; Apollo gave him a lyre, and they say that harps were often carved from willow. The woods have the answer, I suspect, but it will take time to draw it forth.

Friday 25 June

Van in chaos. The lids on the storage lockers beneath the berths are propped open so Sven and I can access the water tank and its system of copper pipes, like an alchemist's distillery – drafts of poems are strewn among the cushions. 'You can read in the space of a coffin, and you can write in the space of a toolshed meant for mowers and spades,' wrote Annie Dillard of her studio in *The Writing Life*. She did not live in her studio.

Sven tramples mud into the carpet, and faffs and experiments, but I am more patient now, having seen his persistence pay off many times. He switches the water heater on, and the red light flickers.

I feel a bit redundant. Maybe I can help solve the problem in my own manner. I open the I Ching app and type *how to fix water heater?*

'What are you doing? Put that thing away,' says Sven.

The divination falls into place: FIRE over LAKE. *Opposition. In small matters, good fortune.*

Good. Yet a note of cryptic caution follows. *Flame seeks heaven, the lake seeks earth. When opposition rules, change can only be brought about gradually. The forces in opposition will resist any attempt to compel them to one course or another.*

The app gains force: *Fire and water do not adapt their natures to one another. They do not mingle except at the cost of one or the other's identity. So too in society there are opposites which can never be reconciled, which depend for their identity on their separateness.*

I do not wish to compel anything. But Sven does. He wrenches out the old water pump. He has bought a new one; the accompanying manual describes it as a 'water pimp'. He shakes gleaming brass terminals onto the muddy carpet. They come from his mate who is doing the refit for Heathrow.

'He said a caravan job was a bit small for him, but whistled these up for me anyway.' The fittings connect the valves of the pump to the incoming and outgoing pipes. 'He told me it was this way up,' Sven says. 'I think.' We switch the pump on. It makes a whirring noise, but when I turn on the tap, no water comes out. There's a nasty wheezing from the back of the van where the Aquaroll cable feeds in.

'I'm no expert,' says Sven, 'but I think my mate got it the wrong way round.' He places his finger against the end of the tap, testing for suction.

'I hope they put in the valves the right way round at Heathrow.'

He unfixes the terminals, and reverses the pump. A dribble comes out of the tap. Progress: water, even if it's not hot water.

Sven has also bought an 'intelligent charger' for the battery under the berth. 'You can put that lot together,' he says, handing me the battery and a bundle of wires.

I unfold the instruction brochure, an epic publication in many languages. 'Look. It says: "Do not cover. Do not use in enclosed space."'

'What did I tell you?' he says. 'Never, ever read the instructions.'

Dan Richards sends a postcard of thanks for my Get Well wishes – he's been in hospital with near-terminal Covid. 'People in Hazmat suits turned up and took me to A&E,' he writes. 'A Covid test which took inspiration from the way the Ancient Egyptians extracted the brains of their dearly departed . . . and then seven days of Isolation.' Hard to imagine Dan, most social of beings, in isolation. But the news is good: 'Lungs like used teabags *but alive.*' He sounds *very* alive – his words swirl across the card in red and black ink, telling me he is writing a book about the night.

Dan's card depicts *Princess Coronation* Class Pacific, a magnificent blue-and-silver locomotive built at Crewe in 1937 to haul the prestigious *Coronation Scot* between London and Glasgow. Only a few years later, during the Second World War, all trains were painted black to conceal their movements. I imagine living here in a blackout, even more cautious of discovery than I am now, as sombre shadows passed along the rails.

Saturday 26 June

First thing, Sven calls. Gruffly half awake and very, very serious.

'You know your battery?'

'Yes.'

'Well, I've been having a little looksee on the internet. Turns out you need to keep it ventilated. Batteries make gas, see. It's a closed battery, but even those ones can sometimes leak hydrogen. So we need to make sure the gas can escape.'

'What does hydrogen do? Is it poisonous like carbon monoxide or does it just explode?'

'It explodes. If it builds up in an enclosed space . . . Basically, you're sleeping on a bomb.'

'?!'

'I mean, thousands of people have these batteries and everything's fine but every few years around the world one of them goes off.'

'As in the Atacama Desert?'

A long freight train rattles past. I can hear Sven shouting *I can't hear you.*

I'm not saying anything, I shout back.

'I'm not an expert on batteries, but we should drill some holes in the casing just to be on the safe side.'

I wonder if we should find an expert on batteries.

Sunday 27 June

Cloudy. No sighting of the wren for days.

Monday 28 June

*About noon we had another rain-storm with keen startling
thunder, the metallic, ringing, clashing, clanging notes
gradually fading into low bass rolling and muttering in the
distance. For a few minutes the rain came in a grand torrent
like a waterfall, then hail; some of the hailstones an inch in
diameter, hard, icy and irregular in form, like those oftentimes
seen in Wisconsin . . . Afternoon calm, sun bright and clear,
with delicious freshness and fragrance from the firs and flowers
and steaming ground.*
John Muir, 18 July 1869

The sullen weather has not lifted. The gate creaks, and hi-vis jackets
of workmen bob down the path in the gloom. A symphony of beeps
from a reversing dumper truck. Its orange light flashes purposefully
over the lift bridge, the day has begun! The Canal and River Trust
is making improvements, turning the sandy towpath into a tiny
highway.

After a month mostly offline, I check the news. Derek Chauvin has
been sentenced to twenty-two years, a new arts centre has been built
in the French city of Arles designed by the architect Frank Gehry
and modelled on Roman architecture, the third wave of Covid is
still in progress in the UK, and – at nine years old – Flora Rider
is the youngest ever winner of the World Marmalade Award. The
newspaper silly season continues against a background of pandemic
and civil unrest. Climate change is headline news. A tornado has
damaged homes in Barking, East London. Climate activists will
demonstrate in the capital this weekend.

So much rain – and it's raining in 1869 in California too. John Muir describes a storm in the 'peaceful woods', which soon passes:

> Where are the raindrops now – what has become of the shining throng? In winged vapour rising some are already hastening back to the sky, some have gone into the plants, creeping through invisible doors into the round rooms of cells, some are locked in crystals of ice, some in rock crystals, some in porous moraines to keep their small springs flowing, some have gone journeying on in the rivers to join the larger raindrop of the ocean.

Muir writes reverently of the water cycle, but the next moment he turns his attention to the gravy-stained 'precious overalls' of Billy the shepherd. Poor John Muir, stranded with only Billy for company in the Sierra Nevada.

Linda is my closest neighbour, although she makes only sporadic visits to the caravan she's parked by the siding. This evening, she relaxes in a deckchair, wearing a faux-fur coat, with a glass of wine and a smoke. She raises the roll-up in dignified greeting. While my caravan is an excuse for solitude, Linda appears to be using hers for diverse company. She may be a wizened relic of the Gates of Hell days. I feel a sense of solidarity with Linda, another independent woman in a van. We keep our distance though. 'I hope my music doesn't disturb you,' I say, and she laughs and it turns into a hacking cough. 'I like a bit of music, darling.'

Linda has placed a few pots of red geraniums around her caravan, and I compliment her on them. 'The garden will look better next year,' she says. 'You have to think a year ahead for gardens.'

Tuesday 29 June

Two fingers of his left hand, their nails broken, the knuckle
engrained with dirt, the chapped tip of one cracked by the cold
of winters, played a staccato beat which was as high as the call
of a corncrake . . . one tune had led to the next, and Félix had
fitted them together like one pipe into another till the chimney
was so high it was lost in the sky. A chimney of tunes . . .
The accordion was made for life on this earth, the left hand
marking the bass and the heartbeats, the arms and shoulders
labouring to make breath, the right hand fingering for hopes!
John Berger, *Once in Europa*

Sparkles is hanging out his laundry. He pegs each sock onto a pink
plastic ring. Thanks to yesterday's towpath development he has
a bright new lawn with a cast-iron sign in the shape of a terrier:
PLEASE DO NOT WALK ON THE GRASS. A square of lurid Astroturf
as a doormat. Flaming red montbretia and gladioli grow beside his
boat. Such tidiness is not easily achieved here on the canal, where
everything soon frays, rusts or gathers dust . . .

I walk up the towpath, heading north. Prerona's daughter Katie
has drawn flowers and hopscotch squares on the new tarmac beside
Marmalade Stripe. 'Out of darkness comes light,' says Prerona,
wearily.

Beyond the bypass the landscape opens up to fields where sheep
are grazing. At Duke's Lock the canal divides, one branch turning
left under a disused bridge into Duke's Cut, while the main waterway
continues north. Behind a snowberry hedge, I glimpse the lock-
keeper's house. Boarded-up windows, and a garden full of black
hollyhocks. There's a row of five deep troughs in a low red-brick
wall, where a traveller might once have paused to water their horse.

I turn into Duke's Cut as the sun is setting. The towpath becomes a cinder track and then no track at all. I follow the bank, stooping low to avoid branches; knotty alder nutlets snag my hair. It's not deserted. I stumble past boats covered in camouflage netting or tarps, boats with mangy dogs prowling outside or leering through the windows – *hello puppy*, I say. A blackboard, with a Buddhist prayer chalked up on it. *Well done for getting to this moment*, it reads. *Thankfulness*. The boats are more decrepit the further I go, until it's a wonder they are floating, and the evidence of activity becomes more violent – an abandoned axe, a pock-marked target nailed to a tree, rough hand-painted signs saying 'KEEP OUT'. I am curious what the natural endpoint of this prohibition and atrophy is. Even the oily water in the cut seems unable to flow. And then – I break into a clearing where two men, one stoned and one sober are engaging in a fierce and whirling debate, like two matadors whose bull has slipped away. An older man is sitting on a rotten log playing the accordion. In the twilight I can just see a gash on his cheek, from shaving I suppose – but the blood on it is caked and dry. He sees me, and it's too late to turn back.

'Oh hello,' I say. The stoned man and the sober man round on me like I'm the lost bull.

'So where does this track lead?' I ask. 'And – do I want to go there tonight?'

The stoned man moves as if he's captive in another world. I doubt he's emerged from his trance for years. Perhaps he's controlled by the plaintive notes of the accordion, which seem to be lulling me too. I wonder when this trio last left this brackish backwater. We don't exchange names, but they are friendly. We discuss whether paths are better worn down or overgrown, and the relative merits of rafts and boats and swimming when crossing rivers, and who the Duke who carved this cut may have been. It leads to the Thames, the sober man tells me, a secret connection between the two watercourses, the natural and the man-made. If you had a boat, you could get to the village where the university once owned a paper mill. But I don't have a boat, and I decide to thread back the way I have come. The accordionist looks me in the eye, stretches his arms wide, and embarks on a new song. 'Fare thee well, lovely Nancy.' My composure shatters: how did he know my name? 'Oh, you'll find you're in all the old songs, my dear.'

He pipes my retreat through the alders with a tale of hexed journeys and stormy seas.

My new friend reminds me of the accordionist in Dennis Potter's *Pennies from Heaven*. More stolid than Potter's epileptic drifter, but similarly prescient. During his national service, Potter was conscripted to study Russian at the Joint Services School for Linguistics, where he met Anna's father. Serge appears as a character in Potter's play *Lipstick on Your Collar*. In those first awkward meals around the kitchen table when I was introduced as the person-who-is-sleeping-with-your-daughter, the one who had whisked their daughter off her feet and out of heterosexual respectability, indeed, out of an ailing marriage, but I was *a poet* so maybe that was okay, and the fact that I'd once kept Potter's papers in my office in Covent Garden – all his immaculate tidy handwritten scripts, what we called in the book trade *manuscript fine copies*, basically the same as the published versions but iconic because in the writer's own hand – bearing no traces of thought, no crossings out, only perhaps the faintest aroma of cigarettes, the equivalent of lipstick on a collar I suppose, a hint of a hint of a life – brought not so much Serge and me closer, but admitted me into the family fold, like a newly discovered cousin who could share their jokes and peer around their frame of reference. *Pennies from Heaven* remains my favourite of the plays, although Michael Gambon in *The Singing Detective* is magnificent, and the accordionist, who haunts and perhaps jinxes the protagonists in the marketplaces of English towns, those places of meetings and crossings, is a singer in the rain, one the detective should certainly be looking for, and a visionary like Gavin Bryars' homeless man under the Waterloo arches endlessly looping *Jesus' Blood never failed me yet* – the same words over and over with aphasiac insistence. What is it called, I asked Anna, when you say the same word over and over again, and she doesn't remember.

Wednesday 30 June

I'm living in an artificial paradise, growls J. J. Cale as I boil the kettle. To London – my first trip in over a year. I've been invited on a voyage through the Islington Tunnel, which stretches for a deep, dank and silent mile beneath one of the capital's busiest traffic routes, the A1 at Angel.

We travel the Regent's Canal on *Freda*, a wooden top hire boat formerly of Willow Wren's fleet. Children wearing bright hula leis wave to us from the towpath. 'This journey takes approximately 11 minutes 43.91 seconds,' says Zac, an experienced tunnel guide, when he is not writing a PhD on punk fashion. 'That's if we don't meet anything coming the other way.' As *Freda* chugs into the cool tunnel, we surprise a mallard who clips our heads with its wings as it makes a break for the light. That's not quite what Zac meant: the tunnel is wide enough for only one boat at once, and small craft such as kayaks are forbidden to enter . . . If another vessel approaches, we'll have to reverse to avoid a crash. It's hard to tell which way objects are moving in the dark, but most boats have port and starboard lights. *Freda*'s crew communicates from end to end of the deck using hand gestures and occasionally this casual semaphore catches a cobweb or startles a bat. I keep my eyes on a reassuring illusion ahead: the sky framed by the dark arch of the tunnel, and its reflection, which together form a quivering circle in the black silk waters of the canal. A promise of escape.

JULY

And still, in the beautiful City, the river of life is no duller,
Only a little strange as the eighth hour dreamily chimes,
In the City of friends and echoes, ribbons and music and colour,
Lilac and blossoming chestnut, willows and whispering limes.

ALFRED NOYES, *OXFORD REVISITED*

Thursday 1 July

Dawn in Camberwell. The luxury of a double bed with soft pillows and clean white sheets. Footsteps echo on the floorboards of the room above, and voices rise from the street. A fox stretches on a shed roof, leaps to the pavement and trots off through the estate towards the Walworth Road.

From the top deck of the number 12 bus to Piccadilly I catch sight of urban gardens: window boxes filled with plastic roses; high-rise hollyhocks blooming in the community 'pocket park' at the end of Elliot's Row. A pale grove of eucalyptus in the grounds of the Imperial War Museum. On the pavement outside London College of Communication at Elephant and Castle, a row of oil cans painted blue and branded with the hashtag #plantsagainstpollution. The shrubs they contain are dying. Outside St Thomas' Hospital, a grateful florist has created an arrangement of pink and white roses six feet high, forming the letters I ❤ NHS. The bus sweeps over Westminster Bridge; at Parliament Square, a protestor holds up a cardboard placard: PLASTIC PRODUCERS PLANET POLLUTERS. A garland of water bottles around their neck. This spot, overlooked by the Gothic towers of Westminster Abbey, was already a place for worship in pre-Christian times: it was named Thorney Island after a stand of sacred hawthorns. Those trees are largely forgotten now, but round the back of the MI5 Security Service building, pilgrims can find a narrow passage called Thorney Street.

Marble Arch is covered in scaffolding. This appears to be one of London's most solid monuments, but in fact it has shifted: it was designed by John Nash in 1827 as a grand entrance to Buckingham Palace. The structure was dismantled and moved to its current location to form a gateway for the Great Exhibition of 1851, itself a response to a time of social and political upheaval. Now the arch is marooned at the confluence of roads leaving the city, a glorified traffic island. Here, where bus lanes swirl east round Hyde Park, a new structure has been commissioned by Westminster Council, in hope of encouraging footfall back to Oxford Street. Dutch architectural firm MVRDV – which creates 'happy and adventurous places' – has designed a 25-metre-high mound with saplings growing up the slopes, and an exhibition space in the hollow centre with a dark infinity room of dancing LED cubes. An unintended pastiche of the headlights circling the arch, this hillock will command an entrance fee for its immersive light installation and view down Oxford Street.

Time to return to the caravan's austere comfort. I catch a coach back to Oxford, retracing the route I took before lockdown – now, as the M40 breaks through the steep walls of Late Cretaceous chalk onto the Vale of the White Horse, I look forward to coming home. This familiar horizon has recently lost two of its most famous landmarks. There's the Wittenham Clumps, a pair of hills named for the ancient beech trees that grow from the shadows of Iron Age settlements on each summit. One summer during the 1840s, a man climbed the Clumps and did not come down for two weeks. Joseph Tubb took with him a ladder and a tent and carved a poem from memory into the trunk of one of the beeches. It became known and loved as The Poem Tree, but as the bark aged the letters metamorphosed, distorting so that the original meaning of the verse was no longer apparent, only the scope of ambition behind its inscription. And now, it has been felled. To the south lies the shadow of Didcot power station, where the cooling towers of the boiler house included one of the tallest chimneys in Britain. Its demolition in 2016 was tragically marked by the deaths of four workers, buried beneath the rubble.

This is the axis of England – 'slap in the middle' as Jan Morris writes – the farthest point from the sea. A place of momentum and stasis. A place of invention and conservatism. It is entrenched with secrets and scattered with subtle acts of enclosure. Students who have been expelled are described as 'sent down' to London, but outside the university the city has a record for locking unwelcome things up rather than releasing them. At Campsfield Detention Centre, a few miles to the north, individuals who had fled war, torture and persecution were held indefinitely behind high wire fences from 1993 until the camp was closed in 2018. As a student I'd joined protests, photocopying petitions and painting CLOSE CAMPSFIELD on banners made from old sheets. Secret detention takes many forms. Not far from here, the Ministry of Defence preserves samples of some of the world's most aggressive pathogens, including ebola and anthrax and the plague, at Porton Down. On a bend of the Thames, at Harwell Research Station, the Frozen Embryo and Sperm Archive holds embryos of 470,000 mice, including 'transgenics, mutants, chromosome anomalies, and inbred strains'. Some of the materials archived at Harwell will never be accessed, for exposure to them is too dangerous. In 1946, the year after the attack on Hiroshima, the former military airfield became a nuclear plant and home of the Atomic Energy Research Establishment. Here, the GLEEP test reactor operated until 1990 – the first reactor to generate nuclear energy in Europe. Harwell was chosen because of its proximity to the river, necessary to dispose of the by-products of the nuclear industry. The Harwell website: 'Liquid radioactive wastes have always been subject to stringent decontamination to allow discharge to the River Thames.' Stringency is relative to capacity. Since 2002 the nuclear wastes have been packed into cement-lined stainless-steel drums or held in shielded containers. In this innocuous spot, the legacy of human activity is slowly burning through its half-lives. But no lockdown can be absolute. What yarrow will grow from the rust on this tomb?

Friday 2 July

It was a great comfort to turn [to] the battered, twisted, ruined tin-pot steamboat. I clambered on board. She rang under my feet like an empty Huntley & Palmer biscuit-tin kicked along a gutter; she was nothing so solid in make, and rather less pretty in shape, but I had expended enough hard work on her to make me love her.

Joseph Conrad, *Heart of Darkness*

Humid. Aislin and I plant rows of baby leeks and little beets in the vegetable patch. Meadowsweet pollen is dusting the air – also known as Queen of the Meadow and mead wort, since it was used to flavour the honeyed drink. I pick the profuse and butter-scented flowers to make an infusion. Be careful of the umbellifers, Aislin warns me, like the purple hemlock in the cool woods which has grown to twice my height. Hemlock is dreaded as the poison that caused the death of the philosopher Socrates. Its mottled maroon stems have begun to keel under the weight of its sepia petals, which Robert Graves describes in *The White Goddess* as 'mousey-smelling'.

Larks are nesting on the common. Their delirious song fills the air, but the tiny hovering bodies are invisible. A glider once told me he'd learned to see the underside of clouds as if they were a pavement, indicating a route forwards on the thermals – these slate-blue and salmon-pink cumulus would make a beautiful path through the sky.

Saturday 3 July

Serge passed away last night.

The last elderflowers are so high in the trees I cannot reach them.

I walk to the Pick Your Own farm in the lee of Boar's Hill. This is my private ritual for Serge, who loved the strange old-fashioned fruits, damson and greengage and quince. How many jars of home-made jam Anna and I enjoyed; soft-fruit jam in summer and Seville orange marmalade in winter, thick cut and sharp on the tongue. The letters on the handwritten labels got shakier and shakier, and eventually Anna was the only one in the family strong enough to lift the aluminium jam pan. I pick gooseberries and strawberries, throwing them together in one punnet. Two teenagers pass me a few rows away, wearing matching hand-crocheted hats that resemble frogs' heads, popping strawberries straight into their mouths.

In Evelyn Waugh's novel *Brideshead Revisited*, Charles Ryder's prim cousin Jasper warns him to avoid Boar's Hill. Many writers have lived on the notorious slopes, including John Masefield – sailor, vagrant and latterly Poet Laureate – who kept bees, goats and poultry on his estate, and apparently other poets. Robert Graves and Nancy Nicholson lived in a cottage at the end of his garden. In October 1921 Nancy opened a grocery shop called The Wandering Scholar in a shed, which soon had to be expanded to make room for more stock. At first the shop did very well, as curious visitors came many miles in the hope of buying cheese from the poet's hands. But there were murmurs from Constance de la Cherois Crommelin (the wife of Masefield, who kept the bees and goats, poultry and poets) that trade would lower the tone of the neighbourhood. The enterprise faltered and in April 1922 the steam-punk poet-shop was knocked down. The young couple was left with a huge debt, which was partly paid by Nicholson's parents and partly by the sale of four chapters of *Seven Pillars of Wisdom* donated by T. E. Lawrence. Nancy and Robert Graves left Boar's Hill in disgust. The enterprise has only a cursory mention in Graves' autobiography, *Goodbye to All That*: 'a neighbour rented us a corner of his field'.

How much can be won in a corner of a field, and how much can be lost.

Sunday 4 July

I read up on species that will flourish in damp ground. Sweet wood-ruff or sweet-scented bedstraw, its whorled leaves once used to stuff pillows, and also to flavour May wine (*Maibowle* or *Maitrank* in German), juice punch, brandies, jellies and jam. A popular sherbet made from woodruff plays a fundamental role in Günter Grass's novel *The Tin Drum* – 'as I can breathe and drum, that fizz powder will never stop foaming' – but it was pulled from the shops when people discovered its levels of toxicity.

I plant other mint species beside Prerona's cutting. Creeping pennyroyal or 'lurk in the ditch', with its sharp scent, was long asso-ciated with furtive sexuality, and relied on to force menstruation before safe surgical abortions were available. (Red and gold tins of 'Pennyroyal Pills' were sold over the counter for 'female trouble' until the mid-twentieth century.) Bugle, with its deep bronze leaves and spikes of blue flowers: one of the old wound plants like yarrow, used to staunch bleeding – it's also known as 'carpenter's herb'. Purple-flowered chocolate mint. Lemon balm, a Mediterranean herb long naturalised in wasteland in this part of England, which bees will love. An old Japanese spearmint which Anna gave me several years ago; I turn the terracotta pot upside down and tap the earth out, and only then discover that its roots have wound round and round, desperate for new soil.

Monday 5 July

I'm covered with mosquito bites. Thoreau writes of a technique he developed out walking, an attempt to keep summer 'imps' at bay: 'Though I may keep a leafy twig constantly revolving about my head, they too constantly revolve, nevertheless and appear to avoid it successfully'.

Message from the assassin: tea?

The assassin has bought an electrified tennis racquet with a wire grill that exterminates insects on impact. As he swats mosquitoes, I tell him about Serge. He holds forth on caravans and cadavers: how a human sees their body as a little house in this vast universe of ideas. During our lives we constantly try to shore up the defences of this structure, closing the windows against rain, insulating against wind, creating a sense of 'home'. When we die at last, he says, the amazing thing is that the house just disappears. All our efforts at boundaries vanish. There's just the infinite cosmos. He drains his mug. As Confucius said, a sage knows the world, but never leaves their caravan.

Tuesday 6 July

There is hot water. After almost a month in the van, it seems the I Ching was right, it is just a matter of patience. *Change can only be brought about gradually.* Today the water runs cold then suddenly hot. I wash the dishes, and make a shower cubicle out of the toilet area with an old tarp.

I have to scrub up as I'm going for a routine cervical screening.

The fact that Anna never registered with a GP on her return from living in Moscow was a quiet, consistent concern through my days. It seemed the years in Russia had instilled a reluctance to sign up to any system with elements of data tracking and surveillance. And besides, she had discovered alternative diagnostic strategies. If one of us felt *under the weather*, she would mutter grimly about 'electrical storms' and turn to the website of the Space Weather Prediction Centre in Izmiran. Magnetograms and ultraviolet solar images, indexes of geomagnetic activity and charts showing the density and velocity of solar wind – the site is consulted by many in Moscow who believe the atmosphere affects emotional and physical well-being. I don't discount the theory, but I go to the doctor too.

Wednesday 7 July

What are you struggling for? What is that vital thing the woods contain, possess, that you want?
Emily Carr

Not to be outdone by Thoreau and the assassin, Sven brings round the 'mozzie killer' he promised. It's a little black box made by a company called Life Systems, whose trademark is an image of the globe centred on Africa. It is clearly designed as a life preserver in places where malaria is a very real danger, not for rural Oxfordshire. The instructions advise against use in an enclosed space. I fear it may harm me as well as the mosquitoes. I put batteries in, and it emits a sinister ticking; when Sven leaves I switch it off and hide it under the sink.

The artist Emily Carr aspired to paint the 'helter-skelter magnificence' of the temperate rainforest of the Rocky Mountains of British Columbia. I lived for a year in those forests, sleeping in a borrowed studio, which I shared with an upright piano and one of Carr's enormous canvases. Her vision of trees within the room and ranks of lodgepole and ponderosa pines outside, canopies disappearing into the mountain mist. In this region, like Carr before me, I learned to be wary of bears, snakes slim and fast as the streams they vanished into, and mosquitoes. This distinguished artist, after whom one of Canada's universities is named, worked sitting on a camp stool, cigarette between her lips, adding dramatic strokes to a sketch on her lap with brush or charcoal.

> There will be sunshine in the woods today, and mosquitoes and those sneaky 'no-see-ums' that have not the honest buzz of the mosquito that invites you to kill him. You neither see nor hear nor feel 'no-see-ums' till you go to bed that night, then all the venom the beast has pricked into your flesh starts burning and itching and nearly drives you mad.

Mosquitoes are not the only reason my thoughts turn to Emily Carr. In the summer of 1933, she wrote in her journal:

> Dreams do come true sometimes. Caravans ran round inside of my head from the time I was no-high ... I had caravan fever, drew plans like covered express carts drawn by a fat white horse ... Then one day, plop! into my very mouth, like a sugar plum for sweetness, dropped the caravan. There it sat, grey and lumbering like an elephant, by the roadside – 'For Sale'. We towed her home in the dark and I sneaked out of bed at 5 o'clock to make sure she was really true and not just a grey dream.

The dream needed fixing: Carr had several animal companions, and added 'a meat safe, dog boxes, and a monkey-proof corner'.

Carr had camped in cabins, tents, tool sheds, lighthouses, boathouses and garages. Now she towed the caravan to 'out-of-the-way corners' where, with oil paints and sketchbooks, and a copy of Walt Whitman's *Leaves of Grass*, she was self-sufficient. Photographs show her in the doorway of the Elephant (as she called it) in a painter's smock and skullcap, one of her creatures tangled in her arms. Two dramatic awnings extend either side, which may have suggested the elephant's ears. Crates and cooking paraphernalia tumble onto the grass – like me, she conscripted the outside as an extra room. I can understand how fond she was of the freedom the van allowed her, how it altered her sense of scale. She wrote: 'After living for a whole month, or thereabouts, in a caravan and then to return to a two-storey house with six rooms all to oneself makes one feel as if one had straddled the whole world.'

Once you've lived in a caravan, can you ever return to the real world? My body has adapted to my caravan's tumblehome,* though I have sometimes felt like Alice in Wonderland in Tenniel's illustration, an oversize girl braced in the flooded tunnel.

All the homes I've ever had are haunting me here. All the potential lives I moved on from – the places I might still be, had my work not necessitated a rambling kind of survival, the art of borrowing studio spaces and library desks. Even my first job, before I left home for university. I was keen to move away from everything I'd known, and so I went to Lindisfarne to work as a chambermaid in The Ship Inn. I shared a room above the bar with Rhea, a former sex worker from Darlington who had come to the island for redemption as I had come to it for adventure. A tidal island reached by a causeway across brackish sands that flooded twice a day, Lindisfarne was favoured by honeymoon couples because the mead once brewed by the monks was believed to promote fertility – and so I spent a summer stripping beds slept in for only one night, and plumping pillows for the next couple, and when Rhea had finished her shift in the bar we curled up together.

Thursday 8 July

Serge's funeral. Just an ordinary day in Iffley: an orange supermarket delivery van negotiates a tricky bend in the lane by the village shop. Those who cannot attend the service gather in the street to watch the hearse pass and to pay respects to their former bellringer.

---

* A nautical term to describe the shape of a ship's hull. In a narrowboat it refers to the inward slope of the cabin, or the part for the whole.

Anna's sister greets me at the church door, putting a hand on my arm: 'He was very fond of you, I hope you know that.' I give her a warm hug, but my attention is with Anna. We walk together under the medieval arch, and down the aisle to the family pew. I feel uneasy about being here, when everyone in the congregation knows Anna's story, and will hold their own views on the rectitude of my behaviour. I came to this tiny church sometimes during lockdown, to experience the blissful sensation of being held within four walls that were not my home. A narrow spiral staircase leads to an anchorite's cell, a reminder of those who locked themselves down willingly, outside times of plague.

There are hints of pre-Christian worship at the heart of this ancient building. Over the door, figures representing the zodiac dance in an interlacing chain, including my own sign Aquarius, a woman bearing a bucket. There's a green man and a sphinx hiding among the roof bosses, and in the wooden choir stalls, a carving of a bird on its roost: 'Yea, the sparrow hath found her a house. And the swallow a nest for herself, where she may lay her young . . .'

Anna makes her way to the lectern and unfolds the printout on which the family have assembled their memories. I hold my breath. Anna says she finds it hard to speak in front of other people, having got so used to talking again with me. How will she address an audience, in circumstances that challenge any orator? She stands at the lectern, her mask a little askew. She was always a nonchalant performer. She looks dismissively at the congregation, then down at her notes. And begins to read the eulogy in a clear and confident voice.

I wonder if the best way to leave is to stay. Had I walked away completely months ago, unable to bear the tragedy and banality of illness, I would have been frozen forever in the guilt of a vanished instant. Here in the family pew, we are all black sheep. Anna and I, and another renegade, her beloved uncle ('Unk') who decades ago absconded to New York. He reads for his brother in a voice laden with emotion the Vision of the Valley of Dry Bones from the Book of Ezekiel, which Serge chose in the days before his death. It's as if the passage on resurrection was meant for Anna, as much as for himself:

> So I prophesied as I was commanded: and as I prophesied, there was a noise, and behold a shaking, and the bones came together, bone to his bone. And when I beheld, lo, the sinews and flesh came up upon them, and the skin covered them above, but there was no breath in them … I prophesied as I was commanded, and the breath came into them, and they lived, and stood up upon their feet.

The priest sprinkles the coffin with holy water from a green sprig and the first plaintive notes of the Kontakion for the Dead soar from the verger's stereo. The congregation stands and I reach out and take Anna's hand, and we clasp hands so long that it seems we might continue doing so until the music ends – but then it is enough, unnecessary and sentimental even, and so I let go. This freedom to draw away, yet the act of holding seems now the essence of our relationship: an acknowledgement of independence, as well as the concord between us.

Friday 9 July

Sun glances through the skylight. My van is a sundial: when you live in only one room you have a strong impression of the way light moves around it. The thunderstorm that was forecast never materialises, although rain fell in the night.

Saturday 10 July

Second vaccine. I've arranged to visit Anna afterwards to discuss The Future. Mine is solved for the time being; hers remains an urgent question with an elusive answer. I throw some laundry into a suitcase and wheel it with me across town.

On the bus I read Kate Briggs' *This Little Art*. 'What to do in this old and untimely body?' Briggs translates a lecture Roland Barthes gave on 7 January 1977, marking his appointment to the Chair of Literary Semiology at the Collège de France. 'Forget, is the answer he'll offer. Forget and be carried forward by the force of forgetting, which is the forward-tilting force of all living life: forget the past, forget age, and press forward. Which is to say, begin again.'

Outside the sports hall, a couple of volunteer marshals are basking in the sun. They spot my suitcase.

'Just back from Hawaii?' one chirps.

'No, it's only my laundry,' I say. I feel very tired, and it's only 10 a.m.

I wait in line to give my details to a nurse.

'Are you well today?'

'Yes, I think so.'

'Have you had any Covid symptoms in the last week?'

'No.'

She frowns at my suitcase. 'Are you returning from holiday?'

'No, it's my laundry.'

'That's a strange address: "Care of Bevan".'

'Well, I don't really have an official address just now. So it's care of . . .'

'Oh I see,' she says. 'I thought it was the name of the house. Would you describe yourself as White British? Please go to section B.'

'Hi, I'm Rebecca. Can you give me your full name? Roll up your sleeve, please. Just a tickle. There, all done. Are you going on holiday?'

'No.' I roll my sleeve down. 'Maybe now it's a bit closer though.'

'I'm not having a good day, maybe we can do this another time,' Anna says.

'I'm not having a good day either,' I say. I slept really badly.

'It's just everything takes so long,' she says.

It is our tenth anniversary, but we do not mention this to each other. Anna has been sorting through her parents' things. She's inherited a rack of champagne bottles, which her mother bought and saved for special occasions that never came. We decide to open one. She holds the bottle between her knees and tears off the foil and I untwine the muselet, throw a tea towel over the cork and ease it out. It's gone rotten. I extricate the damp cork wedged in the neck, and pour the sour wine down the sink. The 2002 Clos du Mesnil Krug opens with more promise, but Anna takes a sip, and winces – it's bitter. This goes down the plughole too. I wonder how many litres of vintage champagne I can bear to send into the sewers of Oxford, but the next bottle is perfect. We raise a glass of 2008 Cristal to futures, when we're ready to face them. Or when they are ready to be made visible. To not laying down the champagne.

Sunday 11 July

Bears have crept into John Muir's encampment and are preying on his flocks of sheep.

It's a long time since I've been to the cinema. Surely the Phoenix Picturehouse in Jericho is the perfect combination of public and private space: I am getting out, but it's somewhere I can have a discreet sob. At dusk I cross the common to my new lacrymaria. Seven o'clock is the dog-walking hour. People bring their phones out for a walk too. There are many quiet conversations among the larksong, conversations that would take a very different form in sitting rooms.

Two small boys run across my path, stumbling through dusty pink stamens of plantain and hemp-agrimony in oversize wellingtons and carrying enormous fishing nets. 'We lost our dinosaur in the lake yesterday,' their mother explains, puffing past after them. 'So we've come back to rescue it.'

The toy dinosaur must be the only thing worth fishing for in this shallow seasonal lake, used in winter by migrating birds. I discover too late how marshy the middle of the meadow is. I leap from one clump of rushes to another, sinking into the sludge. I rinse my shoes in the river, but arrive at the Phoenix with mud-spattered jeans, a costume befitting a film about Italian truffle hunters and their dogs.

Monday 12 July

The water heater is not working. I head to Gail's bakery in Summertown early for a hot wash. It has the best sink in Oxford. I recall the time I spent at Shakespeare & Company in Paris, on one escape from college life. It was really a bookshop, not a hotel, and so when the other tumbleweeds taught me how to live on almost nothing in Paris, they started with the best places in the arrondissement to get clean. McDonald's was favoured, since it was easy to slip into the washrooms there without the staff noticing. We walked the city, subsisting on crêpes and discussing poetry in cafes. It felt like being grown up. The operation of the bookshop, with its apparently more settled, sophisticated staff, was a mystery – but being a tumbleweed was, rightly, not without its duties.

I'd turned up at the bookshop with no warning, a bottle of Crabbie's Green Ginger Wine in my bag for George Whitman, the owner. I considered this Scottish liquor a sophisticated drink and I was certain no one would refuse hospitality to someone bearing such a gift. Looking back, I'm horrified (though not surprised) at my naivety in travelling overseas with no money and no back-up plan. As Margaret Schlegel puts it in *Howards End*, 'Money pads the edges of things.' Fortunately, George accepted the obscure tipple as if it were divine nectar. For George was frugal too. Among other things, he taught me how to clean the windows with old newspapers. I worked my way through *Le Monde* while gazing across the River Seine to Notre Dame. Seeing this iconic view while occupied in a mundane task gave me a sense of great wonder at how easily I had stepped out of one country – one life, even – and into another. The newspaper is a trick I use to this day, but no one knows I'm thinking of Paris.

Tuesday 13 July

There is a shortage of Blue, the carcinogenic bleach used in chemical toilets. I ordered more weeks ago, and every morning I get a text message from the online retailer: 'We are working to fulfil your order!' As time passes these words acquire a cast of hopelessness. Everyone in Britain is on staycation this summer.

Sparkles has cadged an unmarked box of foul-smelling mystery solvent from his mate in the army. I'm not sure I want it near my van. In the end we are all saved by Jack, who has persuaded a chemical company in the Midwest to ship over some cans of naphtha oil or 'Solvent 75'. It's highly flammable, but non-toxic. Charmed at the thought of being endorsed by the traditional narrowboats of Oxford, England, they oblige, and pester Jack to see how we like the stuff.

Jack mimes a broad grin: 'I always use Solvent 75 to brush my teeth.'

I raise an imaginary Martini glass: 'Solvent 75 – the refreshing way to end the day!'

Prerona joins in: 'No more Chanel No. 5, I just dab on '75 and I'm ready for the night.'

Jack: 'Heuch! Heuch! I like my women smelling clean.'

Wednesday 14 July

Rain makes idle circles on the slick canal water.

Each of the canal bridges has an official number, as well as an unofficial name. The numbers appear on enamel signs drilled into the old brickwork, numbers that do not flow as smoothly as the canal does. New constructions must be given an intermediary A or a B, or even an AA. Obsolete crossings disappear. In the shadow of the overpass, the stanchions of a ghost lift bridge haunt the cut – a bridge without its span, an arch of nothing but air.

Now the bridge is being repaired as part of towpath improvements. It is a sophisticated operation; our own lift bridge may become the ghost in time, once the traffic moves on. There are warning signs on the bank ('navigation closed ahead') and a fluorescent cord stretches across the cut like a circus highwire. A team of engineers are pumping the water out. When locks are emptied to clean or repair the walls of the chamber, a hidden history is revealed. Not only the bikes and safes that have been thrown into the water, but smaller objects, like the keys of lucky padlocks, attached to the bridge long ago by lovers. The stonemasons who worked on the canals carved their marks too – a secret signature on the walls below the waterline. Obscure symbols, each unique to the carver, were used to tally how much work had been done and how much each man should be paid. The masons weren't the only labour force. The Oxford Canal took twenty years to build and, when the enterprise ran out of funds, convicts from the city gaol were brought in to dig the remaining miles. The canal was opened on New Year's Day 1790: a channel of free movement forged by conscripted labour.

Thursday 15 July

The most enlightening moments of my life, I was alone, and therefore the happiest.
Agnes Martin

I watch *With My Back to the World*, a documentary about the artist Agnes Martin. Interviewed in her studio, she does not stop painting to talk, as she placidly recommends a year in solitude, then a year in stimulus of company. An artist needs both, she says. And rest, as well as work: 'I didn't work every year. I'd work a year then save my money and take a year off, so that I'd know something – because with painting you just get up and paint, you don't speak to anybody, you don't see anybody.' I admire Martin's calm dedication, her discipline and self-sufficiency – she even prepared her canvases with gesso herself. I want to learn to believe in my work again. I want to bow to it when I leave the room (read: van) as she recalls her neighbour, the Abstract Expressionist Ellsworth Kelly, bowing to his paintings each time he left his studio in Coenties Slip in 1950s New York.

Friday 16 July

I manage to unlock the obdurate safe under the sink. I put my passport in, turn the key. Will I ever be able to unlock it a second time? Am I locking away future travel?

Saturday 17 July

John Ruskin taught fine art at the university, and in his free hours he enjoyed exploring Oxfordshire on horseback. In 1874, he came up with a scheme that would improve conditions for villagers of Hinksey and help his privileged students understand manual labour. He planned to make improvements to a road, laying stones and creating a border with banks of flowers. Among the students who enlisted for the task was Oscar Wilde. It has been debated how late in the day he joined the troop, and how much labour he contributed, but he left this record of the experience:

We were coming down the street – a troop of young men, some of them like myself only nineteen, going to river or tennis-court or cricket-field – when Ruskin going up to lecture in cap and gown met us. He seemed troubled and prayed us to go back with him to his lecture, which a few of us did, and there he spoke to us not on art this time but on life, saying that it seemed to him to be wrong that all the best physique and strength of the young men in England should be spent aimlessly on cricket ground or river, without any result at all except that if one rowed well one got a pewter-pot, and if one made a good score, a cane-handled bat. He thought, he said, that we should be working at something that would do good to other people, at something by which we might show that in all labour there was something noble. Well, we were a good deal moved, and said we would do anything he wished. So he went out round Oxford and found two villages, Upper and Lower Hinksey, and between them there lay a great swamp, so that the villagers could not pass from one to the other without many miles of a round. And when we came back in winter he asked us to help him to make a road across this morass for these village people to use. So out we went, day after day, and learned how to lay levels and to break stones, and to wheel barrows along a plank – a very difficult thing to do. And Ruskin worked with us in the mist and rain and mud of an Oxford winter, and our friends and our enemies came out and mocked us from the bank. We did not mind it much then, and we did not mind it afterwards at all, but worked away for two months at our road.

And what became of the road? Well, like a bad lecture it ended abruptly – in the middle of the swamp. Ruskin going away to Venice, when we came back for the next term there was no leader, and the 'diggers', as they called us, fell asunder.

Sunday 18 July

When I first encountered the Thames it seemed too canonical for affection – too known and owned already, a far cry from the swift, shallow burns of Angus or the sluggish, hungover waters of the Tyne. During the Second World War the bank of this river was incorporated as a natural barrier, part of the stop line – a 300-mile defence drawn across southern England in case of invasion. Walkers still find concrete pillboxes along the bank, cold grey outposts among the herds of sheep and cattle. Hexagonal in shape for an unhindered view, they resembled the medical pill boxes that might hold a kill or a cure. Yet in 1965, Jan Morris described the river as 'so undramatic, so gentle, so eminently a region for weekend anglers with folding stools, Sunday newspapers and patient wives in floral smocks'. I've lived beside this undramatic, silent river now for over twenty years. I have swum in it and kayaked its waters in midsummer and winter spate (it can be quite un-gentle then) and its story flows along with and weaves through mine. It has brought me friendships and adventures. My resistant heart is learning to love it a little. Once the waters flowing through Oxford become your touchstone you realise how riverine this city really is – despite the associations of academic grandeur its name now holds, it was named after all for a muddy river crossing of Saxon cattle – and like

Venice, it is built on islands. Sluices, locks, weirs . . . there have been many attempts to control the waters here, before they flow on to the capital, and yet still, the Trill Mill Stream and a hundred other channels creep unpoliced beneath the medieval buildings, new bridges are built every year, and meadows turn to lakes in winter. John Keats, who took rooms in the city while working on his long poem *Endymion*, wrote to his friend Jane Reynolds that he had found streams 'more in number than your eye lashes'. *Some shape of beauty moves away the pall / from our dark spirits.* Some would have you believe it's a city of green quadrangles, but if you look on the map there's so much blue.

I like public swimming pools. I like the clear water, the regimented lanes, the hot showers. I like swimming very fast, and for countless laps. But the river is closer and safer than the pool, so this summer I swim wild.

A man wearing pink corduroy trousers stands outside his thatched house in the village chatting to a neighbour. I overhear him say, 'Well, it was just like being on an endless holiday wasn't it?' I wonder if he has any idea of others' experience of lockdown.

I turn off the road at Godstow. The river splits here, and flows each side of a mysterious island, on which a stone lion and live peacocks can be glimpsed between cypress and pine trees. Swallows ricochet over the water like prehistoric crystal bullets. Local teens are diving from the bridge, puppy fat already transmuting into booze bellies above their swimming trunks. The river is deep here. I strip off, and slip in. A climbing rose is reflected in the green water. I scull through its pink stars.

One other serious swimmer is attempting slow laps in the free waters. Later, as we towel off, Kumiko tells me she used to sail the world as first mate on a tall ship, but now she lives on a narrowboat. I ask whether those old vessels use modern navigation systems and she describes a night, out on the ocean, when she turned off the satnav and sailed by the stars to see how it would feel. She thought of the Polynesian seafarers who lay in the belly of dugout canoes and used their memory of the swells beneath them to navigate a course between the Marshall Islands. Their compass internal, their charts constructed from bamboo sticks and cowrie shells left at home.

Kumiko invites me to join a swim on Saturday organised by a group of women called the Bluetits.

'We go for hot chocolate after,' she says.

Monday 19 July

I plant honeysuckle and white 'Arctic' lavender and borage, its starry blue flowers little larger than forget-me-nots. Three species of thyme: caraway, white and silver. Gardening is a form of exchange and connection at a time when many people still can't meet. Annabel Dover has sent me some seeds as a thank-you for my endorsement for *Florilegia*, her book on the photographer Anna Atkins. The packets are tiny brown pay envelopes with handwritten labels: *Cornflower seeds from Emily Dickinson's garden, Corncockle seeds from Sylvia Plath's garden*. Like Atkins' cyanotypes, all these flowers will be blue. A friend in Germany sends a packet of wildflower seeds. Before I scatter them, the mix lies in the palm of my hand like minuscule flints and ammonites.

Tuesday 20 July

a book that shall contain a record of all your joy, your ecstasy
H. D. Thoreau, on journals, in his journal

I invite myself to Sven's for supper. The desperation of the lockdown has overturned my cautious upbringing, upset the apple cart of etiquette. The front gardens in the crescent are decorated with giant rainbow pompoms for the NHS. A black Fiat is parked in Sven's drive, the passenger seat protected by a pink cover emblazoned with the words *powered by fairy-dust*. Olga, the home help, is in attendance.

I ring the bell. Sven is already standing behind the door.

'Little Miss Campbell,' he greets me. 'You are extraordinary. To the minute. Are you always on time?'

'Yes!' I slip past him, heading for the shower, then throw my sweaty clothes in his washing machine. I wonder if the machine will take my bundled duvet, a memento from the flat. It is still stained with blood from the incident at new year.

'That's disgusting,' Sven says. 'Just chuck it out. We've got a tonne of them upstairs.'

'It's fine apart from the bloodstains.' Although, seeing the grey and poppled fabric under the bright kitchen lights, I have my doubts.

Sven's kitchen is full of little signs with mottos such as *I have one nerve and you're getting on it*.

'Really, let it go,' he sighs. 'I'll take it to the clothes bank tomorrow.'

Olga sweeps downstairs with her arms full of bedlinen.

'I'm making home-made pizza.' Sven is proud of his pizza. 'It's important to be able to do shit yourself.'

'Like fixing the leaky shower?' Olga says, glancing at the hole in the ceiling, which has been there since my first visit, when we were looking at caravans. She helps herself to an olive, and winks at me.

'Well. Yes.' Sven changes the subject, and riffs about the mosquitoes and the swamp and what will I do in winter?

'It was your idea,' I point out.

'Yes, but we can finesse the operation – we should move the van on to the hill.'

'What hill?' I say. 'There isn't a hill.'

'Well, higher ground then. That way it won't flood.'

I remember how long it took to knock in the supports, the hours spent with the assassin and the spirit level. I think of my planting scheme. 'The van is fine where it is,' I say. 'I'm really very happy with it as it is.'

Is it because the van's got wheels, people expect it to be movable?

'You're very fatalistic,' he says. 'You're like the sheikh in *Lawrence of Arabia*. Did you see that film? There's a boy . . . a boy gets lost as they are crossing the desert. *Mahktub*, says the sheikh to Lawrence. *It is written*, that means don't try to change your fate. Against the advice of the sheikh, Lawrence goes back on his camel, and rescues the boy. *Nothing is written!* says Lawrence. It all comes back to haunt him because later there's a murder, and justice must be meted out by an outsider to prevent a tribal war, and when the culprit is brought to Lawrence to be shot, it is the same boy. *Mahktub*, says the sheikh to Lawrence.'

'That's it!' I say. I've been trying to find a name for the van. 'Maisie', its name of Hither Green days, is too mimsy. '*Mahktub*. *It is written*.' A connection with Lawrence, who grew up (unhappily) in Polstead Road not far from here, the illegitimate son of an

Anglo-Irish nobleman and the family governess. How significant a name would be, in a time when being born the wrong side of the blanket was a disgrace.

Narrowboats must be named when they are out of the water, and so the rare ceremony of renaming is often combined with major repairs. To name suggests hope for the future, but it is also a nod to the trail we follow. In his book *The Pull of the River*, the writer Matt Gaw explains that he named his canoe *Pipe* in tribute to *Cigarette*, the boat belonging to the writer and naturalist Roger Deakin, who in turn named *Cigarette* after the canoe that Robert Louis Stevenson's friend Walter Simpson paddled along the Oise through Belgium and into France. Stevenson's own boat was *Arethusa*, after the chaste water nymph.

The laundry machine beeps. The cycle is over. Rather than wait for the tumble dryer, I plan to take my washing back to the van.

'You can't have Wet Clothes.' Sven is horrified. 'Leave them with me, I'll stick them in the dryer later.'

I'm concerned. The balance of friendship and intimacy is at stake. Sven usually sees me in jeans and a T-shirt.

'But,' I say, 'some of the clothes are delicate. They might shrink.'

Sven is at sea with the concept of delicate. 'Like what?'

'Well, *lingerie*.'

'I wouldn't know what lingerie was if it jumped out and bit me,' he says. 'Don't worry, Olga can do it.'

The cheesy pizza is served with Sven's specialty, honey-glazed roast walnuts presented on a lettuce leaf with slices of tomato. He reminisces about the diners on Highway One on his epic journey from San Francisco to Los Angeles in an open-top Mustang. 'And on we drove,' he says, already far away. 'We saw Henry Miller's cabin in the woods. He wrote all his books there. One of the best books ever, *Tropic of Cancer*.'

'Really?'

'Oh yes. Henry Miller was a genius.'

'Really?'

'Undoubtedly. Of course, he wasn't recognised as such, in his time, and they banned his books. He was just like you. He had no money and he lived in a cabin. He was totally unrecognised until his books got banned. That's what you need – to get banned.'

'I don't think . . .'

'They all hung out in his cabin, James Joyce, Anaïs Nin. Then his wife left him for his next-door neighbour and he moved back to LA. And then there was that guy up in Alaska, what's his name?'

'Chris McCandless.'

'Yes, the one who died in a van. Alexander . . .'

'Supertramp.'

'Yes. There's a great book about him.'

I wish I could travel in time and space and take Chris McCandless a chocolate bar, warn him off those toxic wild potato seeds. 'Well, I don't plan to be found by moose hunters in the spring just to make a good story. Anyway, Oxfordshire's hardly Alaska. Fewer bears.'

But the conversation with Sven plants an idea in my mind. What if I were to publish the journal I'm writing in Joy's Field, like those of Thoreau and Muir and Jarman, whose daily lives keep me company here, whose adventures foreshadow mine.

As the sun sinks behind the trees I meet a man at Goose Green pushing a wheelbarrow full of croissants down to the canal.

Wednesday 21 July

Somewhere on the canal a croissant party is underway.

Message from Sven:

> Your duvet has a new home!
> Gave it to the tramp sleeping by the
> recycling bins
> Hope they'll be happy together

✻

In June there was a sea of nettles. Now there is a well-trodden path to a van door, fringed by ferns and herbs.

The soil is rich despite the bits of broken brick, bedsprings and needles I turn up as I dig. The bequest of those who scratched a living in the ashes before me. And the weeds. It's satisfying to pull up obdurate bramble roots, although I know I'll never eradicate the thick network beneath the soil. The nettles are resilient too. Sticky, straggling cleavers uproot easily, even unintentionally, as the hooked hairs below the whorled leaves catch on my clothes. Also known as *hitchhikers* or *robin-run-the-hedge*, the cleavers' vagabond nature spreads little seed clusters of burrs. The matted foliage was once dried and used to stuff mattresses – and so the restive enables rest.

I consider the form of the thunderstone. Fossils were often unearthed by accident while excavating for other reasons. The term is coined from Latin *fossilis* meaning 'something dug up'. One could make up any number of myths about a star on a rock. Today some scientists believe the stones are fossilised starfish, which I like as much as any of the legends, the star wrapping itself round a soft rock as the next era of sludge descends on it. Others claim they are not the sea urchins we know today from rock pools, but another far more reclusive type of urchin that evolved the ability to burrow into marine silt. They developed more spines than other urchin species (perhaps because they were reclusive?), growing so spiky that Thomas Browne in *Pseudodoxia Epidemica* (1658) refers to them as 'Sea Hedg-hogs'. When these urchins die, they are buried in the sediment in which they lived. What an irony that these stones traditionally used as protection from extreme weather can now be used to understand the ecosystems of the distant past.

It's getting late in the year for planting. I scatter rainbow chard in a seed tray, but it's optimistic to expect these jagged little pebbles to grow into a strong crop now. Also heartsease, the seeds small as grains of sand. I keep the packet of red-veined sorrel seeds for next year.

Thursday 22 July

Construction on the Marble Arch mound has finished. Images online show it scorched by the heatwave and far from ready for visitors. Oliver Wainwright spares no punches in the *Guardian*: rather than 'a lush landscape of thick vegetation, dotted with mature trees, the reality is thin sedum matting clinging desperately to the sheer walls of the structure, punctuated by occasional spindly trees.' It's reported that the trees will be returned to a nursery when the hill is dismantled, and the other greenery 'recycled', but who benefits? Importing trees as a temporary balm is on the rise: recently one hundred oak saplings appeared outside Tate Modern. This drive to put nature on show without creating a long-term ecology seems a cynical approach to the human need for green spaces. By contrast, on the Woodstock Road, I spot a touching scrap of evidence of respect for arboreal longevity. An arc has been sawn into an iron fence, a segment of the railings removed, to allow the distended bole of an old sycamore to grow outwards over the pavement.

A postcard comes first class across town from Anna: a nineteenth-century drawing of a wombat curled into a ball. On the message side she has written: 'WOMBAT!!! love Anna.' I tape it to the wall by my pillow.

Friday 23 July

This morning my eyes feel stickier than usual. Really sticky. I can't open them. I stand in front of the mirror and prize my eyelashes apart. The reflection that looks back at me is bloodshot and swimming with pus.

My phone buzzes. A message from the assassin:

Tea in ten mins?

Sorry can't come got conjunctivitis.

Bad luck. Put pee in ur eye, preferably ur own haha. Works like magic.

Richard Price emails to thank me for writing the introduction to *The Owner of the Sea*, his new collection of Inuit tales, which is just off the press. Good to be reminded of this essay, completed at my desk in Germany before Anna went into hospital. The hero of one tale is the embodiment of nomadism. Life draws Kiviuq on around the north like the ocean current, through adventures and dwellings and sexual partners, even gender and appearance constantly shifting. To be alive, Richard wrote in the book, 'means to change, to be contradictory, to be individual, to be social, even to be mercurial'. Yet his email ends on a note of concern at my own mercurial existence: 'I always knew you were an adventurer, I hope you are not just putting a brave face on it.' I appreciate Richard's kindness and the implication I may be bold as Kiviuq – many friends are less tactful about viewing my retreat to the caravan as a mistake. *Very seductive are the first steps from the town to the woods, but the End is want and madness*, Emerson wrote to his friend Thoreau in 1845, the year he embarked on his experiment in simple living at Walden.

Anyway, I'm quite certain of my sanity. I can look after myself, even down to curing my own conjunctivitis. I hold my Samuel Beckett ('Happy Days') mug between my thighs and piss into it. I should have checked whether it needs to be hot or cold. Maybe it doesn't matter. I unwrap a syringe from the First Aid kit and draw piss up the plunger. I glimpse myself in the mirror, *en garde*. Head back; eyes wide; arm contorted; point ready for its lunge. The tense pose could be a parody of Buñuel's graphic film still in *Un Chien Andalu*. I think I look quite glamorous. The first drops run over my bloodshot eyeball, down the side of my nose, and trickle between my lips. Surprisingly, it doesn't sting. I measure the next dose of piss out a little more carefully, and blink the salty fluid to the back of the socket. After a few more shots, the distress my eyes have been under seems to relax. A train screeches past, the van shakes, my piss steams, my eyes weep. There's no question of my sanity.

Saturday 24 July

Eyes much better.

Rain, after a week of sun. Hemlock umbels droop and turn yellow. The field thistles are opening.

The man who lives aboard *Battleship Nutmeg* keeps to himself. Twice a day he limps along the towpath, taking his muzzled Alsatian for a run on the common. Today, we fail to avoid each other, and I ask the dog's name.

'Rae,' he says. Rae barks.

'She barks,' he says apologetically.

'Most dogs round here do that.'

'I birthed her,' he says. 'She's the same colouring as her mother was.' He's had Rae thirteen years, all that time since she was a pup. I realise I don't yet know the old man's name, but now it seems too late to ask. Rae whines, and gazes mistily at her owner. She knows we are talking of her.

I sow foxgloves, geraniums, Icelandic and blue poppies and teasels in seed trays. Apparently the blue geranium is 'erratic' in its germination. Plant a salvia in the earth on the sunny side of the van.

Sunday 25 July

Derek Jarman notes butterflies on the teasels growing at Prospect Cottage. My teasels will not tousle until next year. Here, butterflies dance among the buttercups, flickering so fast it is difficult to register the pattern on their wings. You can identify different species by jizz: the movement and energy of their flight.

Time to gather and glean. A green tractor is cutting the grass in the meadow. The air is full of the scent of hay. The council hedge-strimmer has passed through the village, its blade breaking old and young branches without discretion, scarring the limbs of trees.

Only two flowers left on the honeysuckle. The sweet flowers attract moths to pollinate the plant, and soon its berries, though poisonous to humans, will sustain birds. Comedians Flanders and Swann sang about the divide between right-twining honeysuckle and left-twining bindweed, both climbing and curling but in different directions. Here bindweed creeps over the caravan hitch head and round the deckchairs and tangles in the pelargoniums. The song encapsulates the cultivated chaos aspired to by garden designers like Gertrude Jekyll: apparently artless rambling borders in which herbs mixed with flowering plants – a stance against Victorian formality for a more natural style, inspired by the traditional ease and abundance of the cottage garden.

Monday 26 July

I keep losing the keys to my van. They disappear under cushions, into the wrong coat pockets. When I can't get into the van through the door I crawl through the window.

Tuesday 27 July

This morning the worlds of water and land seem to have drawn closer. Each leaf has a drop of water at its tip. In the lane green elderberries, green blackberries. Conkers are forming on the horse chestnuts.

Thunderclouds gather as I walk to the postbox for the 4 o'clock collection. The village is deserted. News reports that England's weather is 'tropicalising'.

Wednesday 28 July

Rain. The wild strawberry is sending out scarlet shoots with tiny leaf buds.

Thursday 29 July

The last honeysuckle flowers beaten off by rain.

I go round to the flat to help Anna prepare for tomorrow's ceremony. Her father's ashes will go in the family grave in the Orthodox section of London's Brompton Cemetery.

On the way, I stop at Boots and buy a twin pack of sponges.

Anna moves a posh bag off the sofa. It's the ashes, she explains. Cath didn't want them; Unk didn't want them.

Just the three of them at the burial.

'You don't mind that I can't come?' I have to be at the hospital at eight in the morning for an ultrasound. It's the turn of my body to be under investigation.

'No. It is a small gathering,' she says. 'The funeral was for every-one. This is for . . . us.'

'Yes. The interment should just be for people who are so close they'll want to jump into the grave after the dead person.'

'Exactly,' she says.

We go into the bathroom. Today's task is shaving armpits. I make a lather and take one of the sponges out of the packet. 'I'm discovering the Joy of Sponges,' I say. 'Very helpful when you have to wash in a sink. I'll leave this one here for you.'

Anna has bought a yellow dress, her first new outfit in years. She pulls it on for me to see, and asks me to fasten the buckles of her new sandals with matching yellow flowers on the straps. She throws on a cheap fedora hat. She looks dashing and carefree. She always preferred summer to any other season. I take a photo of her, smiling broadly in her interment outfit.

I walk on the meadow at dusk among the pale stooks of hay. A pair of swans, their legs black as the waters of the river below them, stand on the perpendicular trunk of a willow, preening their breast feathers and oiling their wings.

Friday 30 July

Just after my alarm goes off at six, I get a text message:

> Good luck with the
> ultrasound, hon.

> > Thank you, dear.
> > Good luck with the
> > interment.

Kirsten swerves into the layby in a Volvo that seems to be fuelled by perfume and black velvet. Her hair is a halo of auburn static in the dawn sun. Even an angel, it seems, can be stuck in rush-hour traffic. A tense journey to the hospital.

The radiologist smears gel on my belly. She passes the wand over my skin, then begins an internal examination.

'What do you do?' she asks, to distract me. I tell her. Coincidentally her boyfriend works in IT in the Danish base at Thule in Greenland.

'It's so important ... to be able to rely on communications ... there ...'

The baton pauses. 'You're not in any pain?' she asks, her Scottish accent gentle.

'No. Well, not really ...'

'Good.' She squiggles the baton. 'Jump up, and get dressed.'

'Well, your cervix looks beautiful,' she says. 'But look, here on your right ovary ...'

On the screen she points out a spherical mass, which dwarfs the shadowy organs surrounding it.

'It's often the way,' she says. 'A patient comes in with one concern – and we find something entirely different.'

AUGUST

10. and keep going, because it's important

11. and keep going, because it's alive

12. and keep going, because that's what she believes

13. and that's the way the future is,

14. keep going, because she loves it (I love it)

15. and keep going when she can't do anything else (I dare to)

16. and keep going, because that's the whole idea.

17. That's the whole idea.

DORTHE NORS, FROM 'DAYS'

Sunday 1 August

Today is the pagan festival of Lughnasadh, marking the beginning of the harvest. Halfway between the summer solstice and the autumn equinox. In the Christian calendar, Lammas day. Loaf mass day, when a loaf made with flour milled from the new crop was brought to church for a blessing. Now is the time to weave a corn god, making a combustible body out of the golden straw.

I take comfort from the thought of these rituals. And I have my own. The continual chores of caravan life are a distraction from illness. Derek Jarman describes a dry summer day as having 'a suspicion of rain'. This suspicion prompts me to do outdoor tasks while the sun shines.

A stranger is skulking about, down by the Elsan station. He doesn't look like one of Linda's usual visitors, and I ask her what's up. A man with early-onset dementia has gone missing from a nearby village – if we see him can we tell the police? (She rasps these last words out with heavy irony.) Sounds like he needs a cup of tea, I say. Or a whisky, I add, since it's Linda.

Monday 2 August

Misty morning. The water is rising rather than falling.

I eat my first blackberry of the year. 'The lowest berry – right at the tip of the stalk – is the first to ripen, and is the sweetest and fattest of all,' writes Richard Mabey in his foraging compendium *Food for Free*. This is the one you should pluck impulsively and sample as you wander along the hedgerows. Other berries, growing further up the stem, will ripen in due course, and are better kept for pies, jams and jellies. I have abandoned the idea of making jam.

I sit on the van step with my coffee. Most of my mind on today's consultation with the gynaecologist. I am exhausted from the last few years and fearful of the future. And I think I'm flipping out, making errors. I feel oddly tired. Words and ideas seem to slip off my brain.

The wind rustles through the leaves, and I remember the first days in the van when I was so blissfully optimistic. When it seemed like a new start. What vanity, to take pride in health and fitness after digging all day in the sunshine. To celebrate my escape to Nature in the midst of a pandemic. To feel my spirits were invulnerable, despite the pain I'd witnessed. Now the dashing of hope induces a vertigo. This was supposed to be a break, but now I yearn for a break from this break. Instead, I must rally my energy to keep going. Forget nostalgia and regrets – my attention must be on steering steadily through this present predicament.

A freight train passes. Every steel container graffitied by the same gang in fresh underwater greens and lurid pinks. In which city did these swirling illegible letters originate? A private gallery of beauty and rage – and for a flash of time, it seems endless.

The consultant snaps on blue plastic gloves and gives me a swift internal examination. Then back to her computer, *tap tap*, she puts me on the list for urgent surgery. She sends me off down a corridor to have more blood samples taken by a nurse. Soon I will have more needle pricks than mosquito bites. My blood looks dark as blackberries, the vials are larger now and take time to fill; the nurse and her student sidekick perform a kindly double act, as if their purpose was purely to lift my mood not do my blood. This afternoon, they tell me, I should find a friend who has children and watch the film

Nanny McPhee, which I admit never having seen. Everyone with children will have it on DVD, they say. The idea fills me with horror. On the way back to the van, I stop at Daunt's and buy *Trieste and the Meaning of Nowhere* by Jan Morris. I spend the afternoon reading about that hallucinatory and obsolete city, about imperial decay and the song of nightingales. I write a few letters. Jan Morris writes, 'There is nothing more evocative of goodbyes than the sound, look and smell of trains . . .'

I phone Anna. 'Well, they are on it. And that's as good as can be.' Her few words are almost always the ones I need to hear. She does not advise me to watch *Nanny McPhee*. She tells me she is considering buying a tricycle.

Sardines on toast for supper, and black tea. Storms forecast.

Tuesday 3 August

Sarah Rigby, the publishing director at Elliott & Thompson, is coming to discuss the concept of the caravan journal. After working together through a year of lockdowns on a book about snow, I've been looking forward to meeting Sarah in real life. I reserve a table for lunch at Jacob's Inn. My phone rings as I'm walking to the pub, and my heart jumps when I see the caller ID: Oxford Hospitals Neurology.

The call is over quickly. There's an irregularity in my blood and the nurse requests that I come in for a CT scan as soon as possible to see if there are 'other anomalies'. Can you come today? she says. My alarm increases. I thought everything was delayed due to the pandemic. I don't want to be an urgent case. Nor do I want to inconvenience Sarah, who must already be on her way. We agree on a radiology appointment tomorrow morning.

The waiter shows me to a corner table. There's a stuffed badger on the window ledge facing me, its fangs bared in a rictus snarl. I meet its wary stare with my own. I rub my forehead. My brain has gone numb with panic. For the first time since the ultrasound, I can't summon logical thought. I can't see the scan as part of a process that will extend my chances of returning to health. What am I going to say to Sarah? What kind of hubris was it to propose a book about recovery, when I must have been at such a low ebb? What sort of fool survives in a biscuit tin in the woods and continues to write books and entertain editors? With only a small shift of perspective, as in descending from a treehouse, freedom appears to be madness. I have burned all my bridges and now I will die in a ditch. No doubt this is the inevitable obscure and sordid conclusion to a lifetime of rootlessness. Sven convinced me I was Alexander Fleming, but I'm just the mouldy Petri dish.

Sarah is warm and wise and a little windswept, having chosen to walk all the way from the station. She seems like the kind of person one could explain anything to. I'm sure she would take a poet melting down over a Niçoise salad in her stride, and with compassion. But I have no intention of wasting these valuable hours we've carved out to discuss the book. Instead, I take grateful shelter in our freewheeling conversation about writing and the environment. We speak of access to the countryside, and trespass. My nerves settle. I can't eat much, but the little tomatoes are sweet.

Sarah and her daughter have been fossil-hunting in Lyme Regis on the Jurassic Coast. They found a giant ammonite and some devil's toenails. When we expand the imagination to geologic scales of deep time, she says, little thinking how reassuring I find her words, perhaps we can adjust to significant life changes without catastrophe.

Meanwhile, the long view of the future is also shifting. With climate crisis, humans are mourning the disappearance of a multitude of life forms, anticipating the loss of the rituals and ways of life entangled with them – the corn god and the fern spores, the yarrow stalks and ceramic eggs – and the potential demise of our own species too. The grief is bitter, but at its kernel is the hope for ecological renewal.

Sarah takes the riverbank route back to the station. A few minutes into her walk I get a happy message: *I saw a kingfisher...* Halcyon, the calmer of storms. Will writing this book be the task I need to get me through the unexpected developments in my own story? But I do wonder how it's going to end.

Wednesday 4 August

To the Churchill Hospital. I dress in my smartest clothes, partly out of respect for the doctors and partly to persuade myself I am coping effectively. And it does help me cope. Today I was asked to bring my passport for ID – luckily, the safe was easy to unlock.

When the receptionist opens it, dead maggots drop out from between the pages.

I know I haven't travelled for a long time but this is ridiculous.

'Oh sorry,' I say. She looks horrified.

After the clean radiology department, in which everything is automated – even the voice telling me when to breathe, and when to hold my breath – it is a comfort to be back at the green and filthy canal.

My body's fate is now in others' hands. *It is written.* Who do you tell when surgery is on the horizon? I had decided to keep this private, but I feel an uncharacteristic sensation of loneliness. In his documentary *Griefwalker*, Stephen Jenkinson, the author and culture activist, says most humans are not afraid of being dead, they are afraid of not being carried through the process. Who will carry me? It seems deserving that I should have to weather this doubt, since I was not able to bear Anna through illness or console her suffering.

Yet Jenkinson also describes the relation between mortality and love of life. A reminder that there is much to reap in Joy's Field. 'Grief is not a feeling; grief is a skill. And the twin of grief as a skill of life, is the skill of being able to praise or love life. Which means wherever you find one authentically done, the other is very close at hand.'

Thursday 5 August

Wasps are nesting in the twisted roots of the willow. A young wasp lands on my palm and begins grooming, dipping its mandibles to my skin and leaning innocently on my lifeline. It lifts its stinger and rubs its abdomen with claw feet, then brushes its head which is covered in light fur like a *ushanka*. I am wary of the sting, but to encourage it to move on might be as dangerous as to let it stay. Is this ill health – to know something creaturely and unpredictable rests in the body, and to live along with it?

Friday 6 August

The wasps are in the van. They have found the pot of honey, and stung me on the eyelid.

The hurdles the van puts in my path, and the kindly jibes of Sven and the assassin as we resolve them, pull my attention into the present and distract me from terrifying thoughts. These unorthodox friends are like two sun dogs, those optical phenomena that appear each side of the sun in the cold atmosphere of the polar regions. Luminous orbs caused by the refraction of light rays by ice crystals, brilliant and fugitive.

Aislin and the assassin are holding a tea party. Stragglers and strangers have gathered outside the shed. The head waiter from the restaurant on the river is slicing a crate of melons into quarters then slicing them again; a melon boat for each of us. Aislin passes a box of dates towards me. 'Hello, hermit,' she says. She turns to the table, announcing: 'Meet our hermit.' I smile uncertainly. The assassin swills out old leaves from the teapot and throws in fresh green.

Aislin catches my eye. She hasn't forgotten. She will ask me later, in private, how I'm doing.

Ulf, who lives on *Halcyon*, has spent the afternoon trimming the hedge along the towpath, cutting back the bines of the wild hops to reveal memorials the assassin set up to boaters who have left their moorings for good. I offer him a pistachio baklava, and ask about the poignant elum* painted with decorations in a traditional roses-and-castles style. Aislin tells me it was rescued from the shell of a boat which burned out one night, twenty years ago, with a woman and her children aboard. Further up the towpath, on a sheet of rusted steel, he's etched the name of a friend who was poisoned by carbon monoxide from his heater. The assassin seems tired. I regret steering

* The combined rudder and tiller of a narrowboat.

us into this morbid conversation so I tell him about the wasp nest; he offers something called DOOM. Does it kill them, I ask. He laughs.

I take a deckchair next to Arthur, a young mathematician who researches sequencing by studying patterns in nature. Like starling murmurations, he says. Sipping tea from a small glass, he explains it's hard to understand murmurations because there's rarely enough data. Most people just film on their phone, he says, or take a single photo, but to truly understand the flight of birds – their responsiveness to the earth, the air and each other – you need to position cameras at three points to get a depth reading.

My work and Arthur's have a common element. Chance. He recalls a professor asking her class to repeat an experiment to create a light ray through a crystal, like that on the cover of Pink Floyd's album *The Dark Side of the Moon*. It's very hard to deliberately create the circumstances that cause a wave of light to refract like this, he says. None of us could do it. Imagine splitting light for the first time. And, he adds, it was imagination that led the scientist who discovered ultraviolet light to investigate the 'empty' space after the purple ray. Imagination, and the faith there might be something there, even when it couldn't be seen.

The weather changes, and we carry the picnic table into the half-built house as the raindrops begin to fall.

Saturday 7 August

Wind funnels down the tracks, and buffets the van. Magpies and crows chatter in alarm.

Chard seedlings appear. No sign of heartsease.

To the Phoenix with Anna to see *Limbo*, a film about four refugees awaiting the results of their asylum claims on a beautiful, windswept Scottish island. The men aren't permitted to work until they get their papers, and there's an exquisite ennui, relatable to a lockdown. Omar (Amir El-Masry) is a brilliant musician from Syria, who carries his oud everywhere in its case, although he claims to be unable to play it due to a wrist injury. His grief and doubt contribute to the silence of the strings.

I am also waiting for my papers to The Future.

We go to the Jude the Obscure for a drink, but don't have much to say to each other. Anna calls a taxi, and I want another glass of wine. Luckily, the last shop on the way to the canal is the Grog Shop. According to the sign over the door THE G--- -HOP. It is such an Oxford institution, there is no need to mend it ('Fish sold here,' I think). From outside, it appears to be a regular corner shop, where you might expect a grudging selection of booze: a cheap Chardonnay in the chiller cabinet, bottles of rough Merlot, some broken four-packs of Stella or Heineken. But the Grog Shop's grog stock has taken over its narrow aisles so there is no space for anything else but crisps and the odd special offer. (Today the till counter is piled high with polystyrene trays of golden *gulab jamun*, sweating under cellophane.) Sometimes, you will find a confused new resident peering round the end of an aisle hoping to find staples – surely, some bread, or biscuits? – but discovering only more cans: Olvi Double buck from Finland, Erdinger Weißbier from Munich, labels redolent of nights in Tokyo or Brooklyn. The markup is extortionate. Most customers are wealthy students, all budgetary sense dimmed by an afternoon drinking on the meadow. Evening is the best time to prowl here, when the serious custom is just beginning. A blue-haired woman and I keep bumping into each other as we circle the aisles. There's wine, too – stashed away in the back are classics like Buckfast cider and Leibfraumilch, and plastic bottles and bocksbeutels and ancient jeroboams priced at £89, which look drinkable but who knows? There's anarchy in the wine department – the labels on the shelves are few and always out of sync. Where is that cheap bottle of Corbières for £6.99? That's the one I want, but it's not anywhere to be seen. Some bottles have old-fashioned orange price stickers peeling from the glass. They look as though they've been on the shelf a long time, but without the cellar cobwebs that might inspire confidence. I carry something French and possibly inexpensive to the till. The cashier darts past me. 'She stole that sherry!' he wails, as the blue-haired woman legs it down the street. He makes a phone call to his manager, while scanning the barcode on my bottle. 'Eighteen ninety-nine, please.' I make an excuse and leave. I shouldn't be drinking, anyway. Back at the van, I make ginger tea.

Sunday 8 August

When I first moved back to Oxford from Canada, sorry to leave the studio among the ponderosa pines, I found a job in Maltby's Bindery on St Michael's Street. Downstairs, my supervisor Joan and I sewed book signatures; upstairs, men did the hard graft with guillotines, leather knives, and hot foil machines. So little had changed during the firm's history that no one dared to move a coat hanger that Mr Maltby (deceased) had placed on the hook on the office door a decade earlier. Joan and I had to approach Neville, the manager, and ask for the toilet key when we wanted to go. He timed us, and subtracted the minutes from our pay. I was adept at leather tooling by then, but Neville told me firmly that sewing was all I would do. Joan had come to the job after being made redundant from the Cowley works. She had no patience with my *fancy-pants ideas* on the material nature of the book. She could work any sewing machine at full speed and saw her role (understandably perhaps) as a step down from the furnishings of Morris Minors and Minis. As she ran paper under the treadle, she smoked Benson & Hedges, and sometimes broke open a bag of Hula Hoops. Scattering fag ash and crisp crumbs over the pages of rare volumes, she'd suck her teeth: 'Why do people bother to mend these mucky old books?'

The workings of this establishment could not have been further from the careful ideals of the Arts and Crafts movement I'd absorbed in Canada, or the utopia its founder William Morris envisaged in *News from Nowhere*. Although I loathed her cynicism and her cigarette smoke, Joan introduced me to a different side of Oxford, beyond the rare books and theses. Personified in another Morris: William Richard, who began his career aged fifteen as an apprentice to a local bicycle dealer. He soon moved on to run his own repair business from his parents' garden shed on James Street, first bicycles and then motorcycles, and operated a taxi service too. It was inevitable he would progress to motor cars: Morris Motors was established on a disused military site at Cowley in 1916. When Sir William Richard Morris died in 1963, he was one of the most famous industrialists of the age.

The two William Morrises are connected (in my mind) by forces as tenuous and toxic as Joan's blue smoke spirals: inequality and social exclusion. It was in Oxford that Morris – socialist reformer, writer of speeches and manifestos and protracted poems, designer and printer, traveller in Iceland – began to formulate his views on art and politics. He met Jane Burden, the daughter of a local ostler, whom he would marry. Near the source of the Thames, they created 'heaven on earth' at Kelmscott Manor, a home furnished according to his principles of design. A manufacturer too, of furnishings and decorative arts, it was as an environmentalist that his principles diverged most from Sir William Richard's. He appealed for the conservation of green spaces to offer people relief from toil:

> Civilisation, it seems to me, owes us some compensation for the loss of this romance, which now only hangs like a dream about the country life of busy lands. To keep the air pure and the rivers clean, to take pain to keep the meadows and tillage as pleasant as reasonable use will allow them to be; to allow peaceable citizens freedom to wander where they will, so they do no hurt to garden or cornfield; nay, even to leave here and there some piece of waste or mountain sacredly free from fence or tillage as a memory of man's ruder struggles with nature in his earlier days: is it too much to ask civilisation to be so far thoughtful of man's pleasure and rest, and to help as far as this her children to whom she has most often set such heavy tasks of grinding labour?

The 'misery' that Morris protested, 'the dwellings of man grown inexpressibly base and ugly' in the slums of mid-nineteenth-century Oxford were all too evident in the late twentieth. When I arrived at the university in 1996, the city was poorer than Oldham. One in four children lived in households dependent on income support, and the gulf between rich and poor was growing. The Blackbird Leys estate (where Joan lived, among her begonias and hanging baskets) was infamous for its poverty. Developed in the 1940s to satisfy the need for housing workers at the car plant, it has been described as a 'terminus' beyond the ring road. By the 1990s, many in Blackbird Leys were unemployed. Out of a culture of working with cars, a culture of car crime developed. Young men began to steal cars for virtuoso driving displays in the park and outside the 'top shops' at the heart of the estate. It was a spectator sport – sometimes a hundred people gathered to watch. The group wrote a manifesto (I imagine Morris looking over their shoulders): 'In taking performance cars and making them perform, the joyriders demonstrate the only proper use of all technology – its use for fun.'

It was not all fun though. More seriously, the manifesto stated: 'To live as we choose we must suppress those who choose how we live.' But it was the police who suppressed the joyriders, in the end: the force occupied Blackbird Leys for a week in 1991 and they arrested eighty-three people. Following the riots, speed bumps were installed throughout the roads of the estate. Speed was a privilege. I began to understand Joan's simmering resentment of 'mucky books'.

Monday 9 August

No dawn chorus. One lone wood pigeon. The evening birdsong is replaced by the melancholy, discordant tune of the ice-cream van in a distant lane.

Tuesday 10 August

In the morning I sign a publisher's contract saying I will deliver a book manuscript by the end of the year. In the afternoon the consultant is reassuring but remote.

She kneads my abdomen gently. 'You understand the procedure?'

'Yes, my right ovary and fallopian tube will be removed.'

'Exactly. There'll be a biopsy and your lymph will be checked. I see they've put through the request for surgery already. You should move through the system quickly. You can expect one month's waiting time or even more at the moment, I'm afraid. Please be extremely careful meanwhile. With a mass this size there's a risk of torsion.'

'What is torsion?'

'Any movement within the abdomen could cause damage to other organs. If you feel sharp pain, do not hesitate to call an ambulance. We'll have to expedite the surgery.'

Anna clarifies, later, with the insouciance of one who spent hours in intensive care. 'You could die.'

'They didn't say I could die, they just said I should get myself to A&E so they can operate.'

'Exactly,' she says cheerfully. 'They operate or I. I mean *you*. You die.'

I believed The Future could be moulded to my will, but here I am in it, and it is still uncertain. This is different from the deep vortex of grief I fell into during lockdown. The dismay at my own failings that I saw refracted through the pandemic world. Now health anxiety is a sadistic inner trial that brings no peace. I collapse, like a tent decisively struck on the final morning of an expedition. My focus narrows, to what I can usefully do in the next few months, with energy that seems to be diminishing by the day. My head spins with the possibility that I won't even be able to finish this book. Back at the van, I watch a ladybird scurry round and round the frame of the open skylight, as if in a velodrome. It could escape so easily if it caught sight of the sky. I'm aware how precious this summer evening is, but I spend it with the curtains drawn and my duvet pulled up over my nose.

Wednesday 11 August

Sunny morning after a week of rain. Hazelnuts are ripening a month earlier than Richard Mabey predicts in *Food for Free*. He writes that the tough shell and the fibrous coat that wraps the nutritious kernel have been used as a metaphor in many cultures for the gradual unfolding of knowledge. Here, shell, coat and kernel are smashed indiscriminately by tyres on the towpath.

The hedges beyond Duke's Lock glow with the star-shaped flowers and tight tendrils of wild hops. I wonder if there's a chromatic year: white snowdrops and yellow aconites in early spring, turning to blues in summer, and then these purples: aster, vetch, mallow, borage. When I mention this to Billy Flowers, he tells me I'm making things up. He's sitting on the deck of his boat *Doolally*, drinking a midday can of Foster's. The breweries used to bring their dross to the farmer to fertilise his fields, that's when the hop seeds took root and ran riot, he says. Billy has planted cornflowers and nasturtiums on *Doolally*'s roof, and a pair of fruit trees in pots: a damson and a cherry. There are even stray grass seeds growing from the damp rope fenders. Look! He shows me his single damson. I laugh: I have one blackcurrant. Let's have a dinner party.

There's a new boat moored by the bridge: *Smooth Flow* is painted black and white, the colours of Guinness complete with the trademark toucan. An elegant hound is asleep among debris on the back deck. On the roof there's a plastic triceratops in a cat cage, and a sign: 'No trespassers, we're tired of hiding the bodies.' An open window indicates someone is home. I glimpse a chalkboard, with a summer to-do list:

Pallet Washer
Start back deck
Bike Thing
Kaptcha Washer
Repair Tent Zips
Ice-cream run

It sounds a deliciously simple life. Do your chores, then eat ice-cream.

I sit in my deckchair until sunset, watching the leaves darken against the sky.

Thursday 12 August

I can ramble around here in nothing but my skin, with my hair all tousled. And I've brought no mirror and no way of telling the time.
Tove Jansson, letter to Eva Konikoff, 19 July 1946

Blue skies. I slip out of the van in my dressing-gown to pick black-berries for a breakfast compote. There's a difference in flavour from bush to bush – after all, there are 400 microspecies in the UK. I don't expect to see anyone, but the bolt on the gate creaks, and a couple in white wide-brimmed hats and veils approach down the lane. Beekeepers! Felicity and Veronica introduce themselves as the custodians of the apiary that I've seen in the wood. There has been a swarm, and one hive is now empty.

I'm writing a review of Tove Jansson's *Notes from an Island*, which describes the adventure of building a house on Klovharun with her partner, the artist Tuulikki Pietilä. I'm re-reading her letters too. Last time I read them, I noticed only Tove's exuberance. Now, I see how the strain of isolation told on her during the Second World War, compelling her to keep up a lively correspondence with friends.

Even during the war, Tove escaped to the Pellinge archipelago in summer. Her family would row out to the islands at night for safety, sometimes hearing enemy aircraft over the sound of wind and waves. Often Tove was completely alone for a few months, rushing to com-plete paintings for a solo exhibition back in Helsinki. Early on, she dreamed of living on Kummelskär, writing on 14 August 1946: 'It's the island furthest out to sea, unsheltered, with no chance of fresh water, no soil and no forest. One would have to take lots of bottles of Vichy water, and boil seawater, too.'

In the end, it was the equally barren Klovharun that Tove and Tuulikki tried to turn into their paradise. Tove cut up Tuulikki's old French art magazine to make compost. 'We did many foolish things before learning that it is no good trying to turn a meadow into a garden, or disturbing the shore with jetties which will be washed away by the sea in the next storm.'

I remember reading, perhaps in the pages of *Fair Play*, that although Tove and Tuulikki shared a tent on the island, they lived separately back in Helsinki. Tove preferred to sleep with her work in her vaulted studio. Tuulikki bought a studio in the same building, and she'd bring her partner dinner through an attic passage that linked the rooms.

Wind in the balsam and black poplars at Binsey. It was here Gerard Manley Hopkins wrote his poem in homage to trees cruelly felled with 'strokes of havoc': *after-comers cannot guess the beauty been*. A century on, there are rugged silhouettes on the river bank again.

Friday 13 August

The *Guardian* reports that the Marble Arch Mound has more than doubled in cost to £6 million. The Conservative councillor who led the project has resigned.

Saturday 14 August

The yarrow cutting has taken root in the shallow soil by the railway track.

Katie skips down the towpath wearing a purple ballgown with elaborate ruches.

'NANCY! I'm going to a mermaid party,' she says.

'Are you so. Well, it's stunning.'

'What sort of party are *you* going to?' she asks.

I consider myself through her eyes: my big boots, the oversize fisherman's smock and cravat, the Navy beret. I grin. 'I'm going to a pirate party.'

Sunday 15 August

Late this evening a RAF Voyager lands at Brize Norton, bringing back the first British nationals and embassy staff from Kabul. It's part of Operation Pitting, the codename for the military evacuation of Afghanistan. The news will be in all tomorrow's papers, photographs of this anonymous airstrip which few civilians can place. Far from Westminster, concealed from the media circus, Oxfordshire is connected to the centre by invisible threads like a Bond villain's hideout. Sometimes, knowing this lush landscape owned by university and military, I could believe the whole edifice of the Cotswolds, the sandstone villages and old telephone boxes that tourists come to see, merely a grotesque stage set, akin to those eerie abandoned regions the military take over as a training base for warfare.

After all, the common *was* once a training ground – used as an airfield during the First World War. The first duty of pilots in the morning was to clear the animals grazing on the runway. Not far from the allotments, there's a plinth with the RAF motto *per ardua ad astra* – through adversity to the stars – a memorial to seventeen trainee airmen who died during exercises here. The little toll bridge over the Mill Stream is known as the airmen's bridge, after another fatal crash in which two pilots lost their lives.

I've seen model planes hover above the common, doing loops, rolls and other radio-controlled aerobatics. These sophisticated contraptions have a degree of control and predictability I could not hope for from my van. Is my van just a model house? A miniature version of a real home? As a child I got frustrated by the limitation of toy cars with doors that would not open, steering wheels that did not turn. I asked so much of the replica. Sometimes on the van's more recalcitrant days I feel I've broken into a fantasy that was never meant to be a reality.

Monday 16 August

He was a seaman, but he was a wanderer, too, while most seamen lead, if so one may express it, a sedentary life. Their minds are of the stay-at-home order, and their home is always with them – the ship; and so is their country – the sea. One ship is very like another, and the sea is always the same.
Joseph Conrad, *Heart of Darkness*

Poplar leaves are turning yellow. The air is heavy with the scent of buddleia, a plant that loves to root in the decaying brickwork of Victorian railway architecture. Swifts head south.

It's high holiday season. Everyone is coming and going and there is boat swapping. The canal looks wider and empty with so many boats away. Even *Tycho* the icebreaker has disappeared. The assassin may have sold the old red boat that has been empty all summer, waiting for a new owner. Prerona has left *Marmalade Stripe* in dry dock and bought *Rigmarole*, thus gaining a few more feet for her and Katie; Ariel is buying Prerona's boat when it's ready. Maybe I'll take *Nordica*, I say boldly, knowing very well the caravan suits me better.

Goody and Ulf are giving *Halcyon* a fresh coat of paint. They have inadvertently decorated the towpath with blue drips.

Prerona asks me to water her tomatoes while she takes *Rigmarole* cruising for two weeks. Oh wonderful, says Ariel, wriggling up from cleaning her galley to join us on the towpath. Which way are you headed? Just up to King's Lock. Ariel is planning a trip on her motorbike. I give Prerona my number in case she needs anything else done or watered. Enjoy your exotic holiday, I say, trundling my Aquaroll back to the van.

Tuesday 17 August

Matthew Teller comes for tea, over a year since we last met for a distanced winter walk. He brings an enormous box of 'Luxury' Palestinian dates. We talk about Civil War re-enactment societies (one of his children is a fan), and farmers in Palestine, the olive groves and daily acts of resistance (*sumud*) by people who till the soil. Resistance requires imagination, as well as tenacity. John Berger wrote in an introduction to a book of children's drawings: 'The children taught themselves how to resist. They invented their secret. Their secret was to imitate the air, which nothing can confine and through which everything is visible.' We sit in deckchairs by the tracks, the sound of the overpass in our ears and Matthew tells the story of a local resistance, Alice's Meadow. In the early 1980s, the proposed route of the M40 ran directly across Otmoor, a beautiful wetland. Campaigners bought a field on the route in an attempt to save the habitat. They named the field after Lewis Carroll's heroine, and absurdly, in Wonderland spirit, split it into 3,000 micro-plots. Every single one of the plots was sold to supporters. Faced with issuing 3,000 compulsory purchase orders and going through 3,000 appeals, the government backed down. The M40 took a wide curve around Otmoor, which is now an RSPB reserve.

Matthew uses an app on his phone to identify the destination of the light aircraft whirring above us. There's one for trains too, look, he says. And sharks! I don't want to think about the sharks, microchipped and named, unaware that they have become a proxy for people experiencing wanderlust in lockdown.

Wednesday 18 August

I trim back the brambles growing into the van's air vent, and plant a white currant and a Japanese gooseberry against the sunny side of the van. I'm getting things in the ground as a way of preparing for the unknown date of surgery. Everything keeps growing, while I am on hold . . .

On the other side of the railway fence ragwort is blooming. Known as 'Oxford ragwort', the species was brought here from the volcanic soils of Sicily in the late seventeenth century, but seeds escaped the enclosed plots of the botanical gardens by the River Cherwell and took root in the clinker ash on the tracks. The plant soon spread to other parts of England along the rails. It retained a predilection for soils that had been subjected to heat, rampaging through the ruins of London after the Blitz, along with the magenta willowherb (called *fireweed* for this reason).

Rigmarole has gone. Prerona's giant sunflowers, the hollyhocks and sweet peas tower beside the empty mooring. These apparently fixed abodes can up sticks and disappear overnight, leaving the joy, the wreckage.

2 a.m.: I lean out the window to look at the stars. Even at this hour, a hum of traffic from the overpass. The wind from the north brings the sound closer.

Thursday 19 August

When I was in my teens, I wanted to be either a poet or a haulier. I couldn't decide whether it would be better to spend the nights writing revolutionary works of experimental literature and hosting bohemian parties or driving up a rain-lashed European motorway listening to classic love songs on the radio, then sleeping alone in the back of my truck, dreaming of a fried breakfast. Later, I wanted to be a location adviser for film (my only qualification, a good memory for places). Or establish a business that would invent new racehorse names for unimaginative stud owners. And always, secretly, concurrent with all these ambitions, the desire to be an estate agent. I loved games of Monopoly with the red and green houses and hotels the size of sugar cubes, so easily bought and mortgaged or sold. I daydreamed over full-page adverts for stately homes in back issues of *Country Life* in the dentist's waiting room. These promised a world quite unlike the string of rented dwellings my family flitted between. In the end my parents no longer bothered to unpack, and my father's study was always a box room, that is to say it had books in boxes rather than on shelves, an arrangement that had the added benefit of creating a maze that anyone entering had to navigate to reach him. I have not managed to evade the family curse of boxes, but my upbringing helped me to see that a home can be a pit stop, not a prison, and perhaps like a caddis fly larva a carapace to be sloughed, the more frequently the better. It is no surprise that the first home I own should be both small as a sugar cube on wheels and its own form of country estate.

The idea of naming thoroughbreds for a living might have emerged around the time my parents decided the current house was getting cramped, and that I'd be better off in an attic belonging to some strangers. The 'attic' was in a fortified keep at the end of a mile-long drive. Many such bastions were built in Northumberland during the fifteenth century to function as watchtowers: pyres were lit on the battlements to warn of border raids. The tower had no more rooms than a normal house, but each of them was huge – occupying the whole footprint of the keep. I saw the octogenarian owners only rarely as they shuffled along the corridor between the living-room hearth and the Aga in the kitchen, two matted sneezing shih-tzus at their heels. The corridor was lined with oil paintings of long-dead stallions and greyhounds and red and blue rosettes tacked up with drawing pins. Everything smelt of saddle soap and boot polish. The Major, once he'd retired from the army, had been responsible for walking racecourses; he was the person who decided whether the ground was *good*, or *firm*, or *good to firm* before a race. (This also seemed an excellent job, but not one I could imagine myself doing.) The Lady was an American, and had lived for a while in Manhattan; glints of frustration at the rural life she had married into occasionally pierced her conversations with the dogs or her husband. 'Marriage', she warned me, on one of our brief encounters, 'is just chit-chat.'

My room looked down onto ancient yew hedges, as thick as the tower walls, which separated the lawns from the ha-ha beyond. In summer I could watch members of the family I did not belong to arguing over the rules of croquet. I would sit in the deep embrasure, which tapered gently to an arrow-slit window, beneath which was a useful chute for pouring molten lead onto unwanted guests. But I never had any guests, my only visitors being bats in winter and dead butterflies in summer. I read a great deal and never learned to drive, and I suppose that is why I am not a haulier.

I hang my washing out on a line strung between the trees. Rain. Bring washing in. Blue skies. Hang it out. Midday: walk by the Thames. Crickets still scratch out a song in the grass, but yellow cat's-ear and ragwort and clover are the only flowers remaining. Jarman mentions ragwort as a cure for speech disorders. Heavy clouds are rolling in from the west, and I turn back, walking the shadow where the long grass meets the mown meadow, as raindrops begin to fall. I'm just in time to pull my clothes off the line again.

1 a.m.: Footsteps scrunch on the ballast. A drunken reveller who's missed the last train, walking home along the tracks? A torch beam flashes through the curtain. Muffled voices. I hold my breath. Has the van been discovered? The footsteps come closer. A bass voice starts singing the *Spiderman* theme song. The singer does not know the lyrics, so repeats the word 'Spiderman' tonelessly like a child falling asleep on a long car journey. To break the spell, someone with a strong Welsh accent calls out, 'Suck my dick!' Then the sound of a rake drawn through ballast. Rail repairs . . .

I peek through the curtains and see five or six men in fluorescent workwear, headlamps on their helmets, oblivious to my presence in the dark margins of the wood. If they notice the van at all, maybe they'll assume it's abandoned. On the rails, in the dark interlude between trains, their presence seems as transgressive as my own.

The work on the ballast reminds me of the garden at Ryoanji temple in Kyoto, where gravel surrounds fifteen rocks. The rocks are arranged in such a way that one is always hidden from view. The number fifteen has connotations of completeness in Buddhism; in this imperfect world, the fifteen rocks may not all be visible at the same time. One rock must be remembered, or imagined.

I fall asleep and dream myself a high priest, and Spiderman and Suck My Dick the temple under-gardeners, who will have raked the gravel into bold new forms by morning.

Friday 20 August

Cloudy and cold. Large White butterflies on the buddleia.

Every year Anna set aside one day in August for writing a poem in memory of the crew of the *Kursk* submarine.

On the morning of 12 August 2000 the *Kursk* was in the Barents Sea, participating in a large-scale naval exercise planned by the Russian Navy. *Kursk* was reputedly unsinkable. At 08:51 *Kursk* requested permission to conduct a torpedo training launch and received the response *dobro* ('good'). At 11:29 the torpedo-room crew loaded the first practice torpedo, known as *tolstushka* or 'fat girl'. A faulty weld on one of the torpedoes caused an explosion. The submarine sank to the sea floor, where the fire triggered the detonation of more torpedo warheads. The second explosion collapsed the bulkheads and the front compartments, tore a hole in the hull, and killed everyone still alive forward of the nuclear reactor in the fifth compartment. The crew of the nearby submarine *Karelia* detected the explosion but the captain assumed that it was part of the exercise.

As oxygen ran low, the remaining crew members attempted to replace an oxygen cartridge, but this accidentally fell into the oily sea water and exploded. The crew gathered in the small ninth compartment, which had an escape hatch. Dmitri Kolesnikov, head of the turbine unit in the seventh department, and one of three surviving officers, apparently took charge.

Kolesnikov wrote two notes. The first, written an hour and forty-five minutes after the second explosion, contained a private note to his family and, on the reverse, information on their situation and the names of those in the ninth compartment. The handwriting appears normal, indicating the sailors still had some light. *It's 13:15. All personnel from section six, seven, and eight have moved to section nine, there are 23 people here. We feel bad, weakened by carbon dioxide . . . Pressure is increasing in the compartment. If we head for the surface we won't survive the compression. We won't last more than a day.*

Kolesnikov wrote the second note at 15:15. His writing is extremely difficult to read. *It's dark here to write, but I'll try by feel. It seems like there are no chances, 10–20%. Let's hope that at least someone will read this. Here's the list of personnel from the other sections, who are now in the ninth and will attempt to get out. Regards to everybody, no need to despair. Kolesnikov*

Saturday 21 August

I dream I'm at a party in a dimly lit room. A cordial made from rosehips is served to guests, and a woman hands two vials of it to me. The test tubes slip from my hands to the ground and shatter, and among the glass fragments the rosehips, still whole, glimmer on the stone floor.

I mention the rosehips in an email to Charlotte Du Cann. She replies with gusto:

> Rosehips are just fab dried and made into a tea. It's a bit fiddly as you need to cut them in half and when dried shake out the seeds and fluff but it's well worth it. Some folk wait until they have been bletted with the frost and gone sweet. For tea you need to steep or simmer the hips, and if you like, add hibiscus flowers. I put whole pricked rosehips in vinegar and leave for a month or two – and also gin (!) with sloes and damsons. I am in love with sweet briar rose this year (the leaves are fragrant and the hips are very elegant). I've never dreamed of them though.

I decide to consult a herbalist. Katie Reid listens carefully to my account of the events of the last year, and makes a tincture to strengthen the body for surgery and support healing afterwards. It arrives in a brown glass bottle with a label on which are written the names of species growing around me in the wood, cleavers and gingko, dandelion and hawthorn, as well as ginger and calendula. Hawthorn is from the rose family, Katie tells me, which helps the body move on after a time of change and grief, and directly supports the heart. She warns that the medicine will taste bitter. We will have another conversation after the surgery. I am crossing a stream using clumps of moss. She does not offer false reassurance, but her presence is reassuring.

Sunday 22 August

Some mornings I am a vessel that has hairline fractures running through it – I have to hold my poise gently, to avoid all the pieces falling, to avoid spilling. The pain of being in the world is almost unbearable, at the same time as I want more than ever to hang on to life. In the last few years I have seen how swiftly everything can be snatched away.

The gas runs out as I am boiling the kettle for coffee. The padlock on the hold has rusted and when I break into it, I can't switch the hose over from the empty canister to the full one. Everything is intransigent. No coffee, again. I slope back into the van and slam the door and the hurricane lantern falls from its hook, knocking the tray of rainbow-chard seedlings off the windowsill.

FUCK.

I stare in fury at the upended pots, the bent and tender stalks, as if they symbolise the total ruination of my life. Compost scatters across the berths and the floor of the van. It is embedded in the Bavarian sheepskin, gathers in the button tufts of the old cushions. I pick it up in handfuls, and stuff it back into the pots along with the hopeless seedlings. I balance the tray on the sink, under the faded Caravan Club sticker; there's nowhere else to put it. I could shake the blanket out the door, that's one way to eject some of the soil, so I do, and then hang it over the door to air, and then I shake out the sheepskin, and all the dust it has accumulated in a big cloud, and throw it over the deckchair, and now the floor is revealed, the carpet into which the assorted grit and leaves of the last few weeks has been crushed, and so I get the dustpan and sweep up everything, until it is clear, and then I open the window to let some air in, and now I've taken almost everything off the berth, for the first time in weeks, I think, I might as well look in the locker underneath, where the water heater is, for Eleanor's book on spiders, which I wanted to send Sally. And there it is! And it is so cold these mornings I could get the yellow jumper that Kaddy gave me, which she says is like a hug, out of the suitcase, and going through the suitcase I see clothes I once wore to readings, the sequined jacket, silk shirts, my pristine white Saucony trainers. Look, there's a space in one corner of the locker – I'll chuck in some of the bulky objects I've been tripping over. When I've replaced the cushions on the berth, I feel content. The seedlings are wrecked for sure, but there is more to life than rainbow chard.

Sven said, you can just turn up any time. I hope he meant it.

There will be a gruff greeting. And coffee, at last. And a second breakfast. Franz Kafka was also a devotee of the *Gabelfrühstück*. Today's *Gabelfrühstück* will be a croissant. There are always croissants in the crescent.

I walk the verge of the dual carriageway. *Morning!* calls a cyclist kitted out in Lycra.

'Oh, it's you,' says Sven. 'I thought it was the boys in blue. I saw your duvet in front of M&S in Summertown the other day. It's on tour.'

He hands me a small cardboard box on which retro lettering reads GET A GRIP: GENTLEMEN'S HARDWARE. Inside is a seductively heavy combination tool: a micro-adjustable spanner with a selection of knives and detachable screwdriver bits, perfect for vanquishing gas canisters and fiddling with fuses. I have been promoted from Worzel Gummidge to James Bond.

'For your O-rings,' he says.

'What?'

'You don't know about O-rings? The Space Shuttle *Challenger* disaster?'

'No.'

'You haven't heard of Feynman? *What Do You Care What Other People Think?* Winner of the Nobel Prize for his work on quantum electrodynamics?'

Sven is nostalgic about his studies at Caltech in Los Angeles, on a research scholarship from a drug company. Richard Feynman, the long-time professor of physics, was his hero. As he packs coffee into the Bialetti filter, Sven explains Feynman's involvement in the investigation of the *Challenger* disaster, a tragedy that mystified NASA experts. Feynman's experiments showed how infinitesimal O-rings in the shuttle's rocket boosters could have failed due to cold temperatures on the morning of the launch. This failure came to be regarded as the primary cause of the shuttle's dramatic destruction 73 seconds after lift-off. But Sven's most enduring memory of Feynman is not his scientific prowess or media stardom, rather the fact he would leave his nook in the marble halls at Caltech, curious to discover other Californias. One of his chosen haunts was a commune, where hippies played drums late into the night. 'The problem with most people,' Sven says, 'is they have no curiosity. They become bankers or estate agents or run-of-the-mill quantum physicists then they suddenly find they've pissed away their life. Feynman was curious about *everything*. And that makes a great scientist.'

I feel for Sven, once part of the arcadia of Californian academia, with the potential for a brilliant biochemistry career, now shuttling between an unofficial care home with giant washing machines and a self-destructing caravan by the canal.

'*Hay que sufrir*,' he shrugs. 'You have to suffer.'

It's an opening to tell him what's been going on.

He takes my news in his stride. 'You can't recover from major surgery in a caravan.'

'But it's my home.'

'It's only been your home for a couple of months, numpty. Come and stay in the summerhouse.' Once he gets an idea, he doesn't relinquish it easily.

'I know, I know – I can watch the grebe on the lake from my bed . . .'

'We're all set up for medical emergencies. You name it, we have it. Round-the-clock care or neglect. Hoists, hospital mattresses, catheters. I even have those dressings the SAS use to stop wounds haemorrhaging . . .'

'I don't think I'm going to haemorrhage . . .' I know I need the van to recover. I will miss my tumblehome smelling of cinnamon and sardines and Solvent 75. But that reminds me – will I be able to do the chores?

'Okay. Just for a couple of nights.'

Monday 23 August

The *Guardian* reports that Maersk is investing £1 billion to speed up its switch to carbon-neutral operations. It has ordered eight container vessels powered by traditional bunker fuel and methanol. The new vessels will save more than a million tonnes of carbon emissions a year by replacing older fossil-fuel-driven ships. The vessel order, placed with South Korea's Hyundai Heavy Industries, is the single largest step taken so far to decarbonise the global shipping industry, which is responsible for almost 3 per cent of the world's greenhouse gas emissions.

Tuesday 24 August

Ariel is coming for dinner. I pull up a row of beetroot, and scrub the earth from their tough skins. A handful of steak goes in the pan (a trick Anna taught me), some pickles and vinegar for depth and sharpness. A spoonful of sour cream in each bowl. I still have no plates, so I use the cracked, chipped saucers that sat under plant pots in the old flat for rye bread. Cooking in the van is a discipline. Most recipes need adaption – I'm becoming expert in one-pot dishes. Would cooking outdoors work better? The food writer Caroline Eden includes a recipe for lamb chops with sour cherry sauce, from the mountains of Azerbaijan, in her book *Samarkand*. She writes: 'Resourceful people, lacking cooking utensils, once cooked their meat between hot stones. Not just any stones, apparently they would select stones weathered by thunder storms, which somehow made them stronger.'

I remember the bottle of noyau and pull it out from under the berth. I take a tentative sip. With the addition of sugar and a dash of brandy, it makes a thick, sweet spirit. Richard Mabey says the gin should be tinted with 'the brilliant green of the leaves', tasting slightly like sake.

Wednesday 25 August

Love brings many surprises and the biggest surprise of falling in love with Anna was discovering that I could enjoy watching pro cycling. This is the first summer of many I have not seen the Tour de France highlights on TV. One year, Le Depart was from Yorkshire, and we went to Limehouse in East London to cheer the riders on their way to the Channel. We waited behind cordons on the bank of the Thames, looking expectantly into an empty underpass for several hours, and eavesdropping on other spectators' conversations. Then the unsmiling motorbike marshals appeared, and a moment later the breakaway riders flashed past, ahead of the peloton, and we could make out nothing but their urgency. The peloton barely registered on my sight. Was that it? I asked when they had gone.

Thursday 26 August

Another cloudy day. I cut back the lavender. The glade is full of its scent. I turn over the leaves of the wild strawberry and find one ripe berry. Pennywort is spreading in the shade.

I sleep all the afternoon and wake not knowing where I am and feeling my mind washed clean. I open my eyes to see a spider repairing its web, huge-bellied against the indigo sky. Here I can sleep away everybody and everything. I can sleep into a new world, then I can sleep away the world.

1 a.m.: Sound of heavy boots on ballast and orders shouted in a Scouse accent. Railworks again. I peer cautiously around the curtain. Orange jackets loiter here and there. Repairing the railway line seems to be an art of discussion and adjustment. One orange jacket appears to be pushing a tea trolley to and fro along the rails. Huge wheels grind along the opposite track going north at walking pace, and smaller carriages marked SCRAP METAL ONLY scuttle along the top, wheels upon wheels. Yellow on yellow. A kind of inferno. Sounds

of tapping, tinkling, revving, a horn toots once, toots twice. No way will I get back to sleep. I boil the kettle to make mint tea. *Chug chug.* A sporadic siren. The little train rolls along the top of the other again. Magic! *Pum-pa-pum-pum. Toot toot . . .*

Friday 27 August

'You might just as well say,' added the Dormouse, who seemed to be talking in his sleep, 'that "I breathe when I sleep" is the same thing as "I sleep when I breathe"!'
Lewis Carroll, *Alice's Adventures in Wonderland*

Morag comes for tea, and brings a gooseberry sponge cake. When she leaves I go to bed. I have so little energy – I should be making more of the days. Wasn't I supposed to be writing a book? I'm mesmerised by the news, which shows a short film on a loop of the latest evacuation flight taking off down a Kabul runway, hot yellow sky, grey mountains. Carrying people to freedom (though never enough of them). Different news channels show different planes, but always hope in the ascent.

Saturday 28 August

The water pump Sven installed is as unpredictable as the old one. I haven't showered for days. If it's all I achieve today, I need to wash, so I stir myself to go to the standpipe for water, then heat a hedonistic amount in the largest Alluflon pan over the stove and wash in the sink ('Joy of Sponges'). The windows steam up inside while rain streams down outside. The van grows warm and muggy from the gas.

Feeling clean and protected from the elements lifts my gloom. I brew tea and eat the last piece of Morag's gooseberry sponge. Whatever tomorrow holds, this moment is delicious.

Sunday 29 August

It is suggested that the blue is darkest when reflected from the most agitated water because of the shadow (occasioned by the inequalities) mingled with it. Some Indians of the north have but one word for blue and black, and blue with us is considered the darkest colour, though it is the colour of the sky or air. Light, I should say was white, the absence of it, black. Hold up to the light a perfectly opaque body and you get black, but hold up to it the least opaque body, such as air, and you get blue. Hence you may say that blue is light seen through a veil.
Henry David Thoreau, *Journal*

The canal is a collector. Its opaque waters a tincture of oil, goose-down, leaves and seeds. It collects reflections too. A rocking mirror backed by mud not mercury, in which everything is agitated. Willows widen, aspens shiver. Black ruptures to blue and melds back to black. The cross on the spire of St Barnabas trembles, windows replicate – windows which in turn replicate the world. We ignore these impressions, content to see only the substance and not the shimmer of reverie. Here comes a house without foundations, a house that can pass through a lock. A lock to which everyone has the key. Skelfs of sky and spire, window and water, shift together and apart as the prow churns through the deep dull cut, and the passengers are unaware they have provoked chaos among these shadows because movement is constant chaos. Yet water is no less real when it is in ripples. Though it can no longer hold the reflection of a house it can still support a boat.

Monday 30 August

I wheel my Aquaroll to the standpipe.

Katie hears the squeak of the tap and waves through the boat window. 'NANCY!' she calls and runs down the towpath. Her tiara sparkling in the morning sunlight.

'Katie! That's a very beautiful dress,' I say. 'Are those real diamonds?'

'Yes. I've got a flower for you.'

'It's the same colour as your dress! Did you grow it on your boat?'

She nods.

'Do you know what it's called?'

'It's a Giant Daisy,' she says confidently.

'It will look lovely in my van. Come and visit soon.'

Katie has already mastered the tactful rebuttal. 'I will. But just now I'm having breakfast.'

Tuesday 31 August

I call my mother to find out what our relatives died of. It's a question I've been unable to answer when the doctors ask.

'Hello?' she answers the phone suspiciously. 'Well, this is a nice surprise. I've just spent the day in A&E.'

'Oh no. What happened?'

'I was in my studio, adjusting the treadles of the loom, and I'd put an ebony ashtray that someone had given my grandfather years ago up on one of the joists, just to weigh down the warp, and it slipped off and hit me on the head. I was all right, but I must have been bleeding horribly and the nice young girl in the studio next door called an ambulance for me.'

Maternal Grandmother: heart attack; Maternal Grandfather: old age; Mother: ebony ashtray. My list for the doctor has narrowly escaped sounding like a game of *Cluedo*.

'Was there anything else, darling? It's just that Monty Don is on.'

'They'd find a name for it,' says Sven, when I tell him. 'Brain haemorrhage, probably.'

SEPTEMBER

Human beings do not go hand in hand the whole stretch of the way. There is a virgin forest, tangled, pathless, in each; a snow field where even the print of birds' feet is unknown. Here we go alone, and like it better so. Always to have sympathy, always to be accompanied, always to be understood would be intolerable.

VIRGINIA WOOLF, 'ON BEING ILL'

Wednesday 1 September

Sven is awful, the van is awful. I hate Sven. His chiding is beginning to erode my (already dented) confidence. I don't mind being told how to change a gas cylinder but I am weary of him telling me I'm approaching my life wrong. How dare he criticise my working methods. *There's no money in poetry. You need to cause a scandal.* The van has become a stained portolano of the summer's crises: the battery-bomb and the leaking water tank under my berth, the tangled wires of the intelligent charger hanging over it. There's no space or time for my work. I'm exhausted. The constant shuttling around and worry about the various ways my home is falling apart is making things shaky underfoot. Do I need Sven to make the van work? Every time one problem is solved another seems to emerge. In darker moments I notice the problems seem to emerge in the areas where Sven has just fixed something else. Could he be *breaking* my van, not fixing it?

Sven infuriates me, but he has a knack of appearing when I am at my lowest ebb, when everything seems lost. I'm curled up in bed in the middle of the day, weary and fretful, when he phones to say he's going to the supermarket and do I need anything. I'm so glad to hear a kind voice I burst into tears. He's surprised. I'm surprised. We don't really have this kind of friendship. Things get fixed, but no *emotion* is shown on either side.

'Something's up,' he says. 'I'm coming to bail you out.'

Back in suburbia, Sven prints off the symptoms of carbon monoxide poisoning from the NHS website while I loll on the couch.

'There you are. Emotional, tick. Tired, tick. Confused, tick. Headache, tick. Impulsive and irrational decisions, tick. Are you short of breath?'

'Yes, something like apnoea. As if my lungs have hiccups. I thought that was post-Covid.'

'Oh man. That's classic carbon monoxide, you don't know you're breathing it. They call it the silent killer. Says here it causes fits, brain damage, nerve damage and death.'

He wolfs a croissant. In one of his former lives, between the music studio and the cigar-dealing, he worked in a morgue. 'I used to source the brains of people who'd died of carbon monoxide poisoning from hospitals. So the lab could use them for research.'

Of course he did.

'I got to know all the doctors, so they'd call me up when they had a fatal CO case.'

'Was that even legal?'

'It wasn't illegal, no . . . not at the time. Anyway, I found out a lot about CO. When it gets into your bloodstream, the molecules hitch a ride on the haemoglobin, that's the red blood cells that carry oxygen around your body. So it boots off the oxygen, and without oxygen reaching your body the cells and tissue fail and die. That's why you've been feeling so tired . . . and acting so fucking weird.'

That – and everything else, I think. There were plenty of other reasons to feel weird, but apparently it was just the wrong molecules.

'You better stay here for a couple of days. We'll look after you. No more fits and fatigue. I'll put a mattress in the summerhouse.'

Thursday 2 September

At 10 o'clock Sven is just embarking on breakfast. 'My mam dreamed my dad was dead last night.'

'Oh dear god.' I put my head in my hands.

'You say that, but you get to know us here, you have to laugh. A few nights ago she called me in to tell me the floor had melted away in the corner of the room.'

Olga is taking a break before starting work. She scrolls through her phone. 'Look, there's a company in Japan you can pay when you want to disappear. They'll arrange everything. Cover your trail. Give you a new name.'

I fill the giant Bialetti at the sink. Sparrows are hopping about under the rowan. So many sparrows come to the feeders that the neighbours have begun to ask if Sven's birdseed is magic. In fact, it's the cheapest seed at the garden centre. Why not tell them it's magic? I ask. You could bag it up and sell it at a profit. Surprisingly, he doesn't go for this venture. Maybe he's too proud of his plump sparrows.

A shadow flickers past the window, and drops into the beech hedge. There's a startled *peep*, then silence.

'That's nature for you,' Sven says. 'Red in tooth and claw. Sparrowhawk spots its breakfast and whoomph . . .'

'*Squeak.*'

'Oh, you'd squeak all right.'

'No more little sparrow.'

'Little sparrow is dead. *Death in the Hedge*. Ha! Now that's a good title for your book. Better than *Thunderball* or whatever.'

❋

An ambulance brings Sven's dad back from hospital, where he's had a pacemaker fitted.

Dennis lifts his polo shirt and shows off the scar on his pale chest.

'Very impressive bruise,' I say. 'Well done.'

'Show her your scar for carotid cancer,' Sven says.

Dennis obediently pulls down his collar.

'My dad had *proper* cancer,' Sven says. 'Not like your … bunion.'

I scowl at him.

'I remember the consultant – he brought in all the medical students, and told them to take a good look as this was one of only four cases ever known in the UK. My dad asked, *What happened to the other three?* And the consultant answered, *They all died.* The medical students looked like they wanted to sink through the floor. But see, my dad's a survivor.'

After supper, we watch *Heimat* on DVD. The protagonist Jakob longs to escape his grey village and is learning about South America, where the indigenous languages have twenty-two words for the colour green. The monochrome palette is heightened by occasional colourisation, which accentuates a copper lamp, a bright silk dress. I miss the subtle shades of the woods. It's time to go back to the van.

Friday 3 September

'Do you think this was all a big mistake?' I have a suspicion the van is trying to kill me.

'You wanted an old van,' Sven says. 'It's like an old car. You just have to tinker with it. We'll get there. We're sorting out your life.'

We drive back to the woods with a Fire Angel – a device that gives a detailed reading of parts per million of carbon monoxide in the air. It will help investigate whether I need a new stove. I take the burners off the hob and light the gas. Enormous blue and orange flames leap up to the ceiling.

Within seconds the reading rises from zero to 30 ppm, then to 100 ppm.

'Good grief,' says Sven, and looks at me in grim assessment. 'You've been breathing this in all summer.'

Every time I make a cup of tea.

The escalating measurements remind me of the way people are beginning to mark time in the Anthropocene, by the concentration of atmospheric carbon dioxide. When the Ok glacier in Iceland was declared extinct, and a memorial service was enacted for it in August 2019, the date was given using the global atmospheric carbon dioxide reading of 415 ppm. Glacial ice holds deep histories, including a record of the levels of CO_2 in past atmospheres: during the Industrial Revolution, the figure was roughly 290 ppm. As higher temperatures and reduced snowfall cause glaciers to retreat, the information in these ancient archives is lost.

Our investigations on the stove are more simple, but they don't resolve anything. At least with the Fire Angel I'll be able to keep track of the air I breathe. When Sven has gone, I sit out under the willow. I still feel weary. A heron flies down the tracks, in the direction of the city, like a plane coming in to land. On the branch above me the robin chitters and looks at me keenly. I silently promise it mealworms.

✳

Aislin plans to coppice the willows. The stems will be cut back down to the ground this winter, to encourage new shoots next spring.

John Evelyn mentions the 'promiscuous' types of willow:

> the common-white willow, the black, and the hard-black, the rose of Cambridge, the black-withy, the round-long sallow; the longest sallow, the crack-willow, the round-ear'd shining willow, the lesser broad-leav'd willow, silver sallow, upright broad-willow, repent broad-leav'd, the red-stone, the lesser willow, the strait-dwarf, the long-leav'd yellow sallow, the creeper, the black-low willow, the willow-bay, and the ozier.

The slim yellow leaves of the crack willow are everywhere. It is the tree of resurrection. Charlotte Du Cann writes how the limbs 'break and snap off, but wherever a part falls down seemingly dead, it sprouts roots and jumps up miraculously to life again'. The lost and broken limbs often drift downriver, until they catch in the bank and generate new trees, hence their Latin name *salix*, from *salire* meaning 'to jump'. I've seen the craggy, split boughs sunk in the river, never until now realising this damage is part of the willow's plan. This plant that revives so swiftly from injury is a remedy for the human body too. Charlotte continues: 'Salicylic acid, the basis of aspirin (originally taken from white willow bark), encourages flow and releases the dammed-up energies that cause pain in our heads and joints.'

Saturday 4 September

I'm reading Stephen Rutt's new book *The Eternal Season*. He writes that 'no matter how warm the planet gets the amount of light a place receives is unchanging'. This dose of sunlight, or the photoperiod, is crucial to the changing seasons: trees let sap rise or leaves fall, birds use it to judge when to migrate or stick. Many passerines have now flown south. In the 1920s, Earl Grey described the song of the chiffchaff in September as 'a subdued repetition ... a sort of quiet farewell'. Rutt writes that as climate changes, sometimes the chiffchaff chooses to overwinter here – but the decision to stay may yet prove fatal.

The robin hopped in through my door this morning; I gave it a raisin. Dorothy Wordsworth had a pet robin, which 'cheared my bed-room with its slender subdued piping'.

Someone has mown the grass at Duke's Lock. Windfalls tumble to the ground and lie under the crab apple trees, their golden skin mottled with dark spots. Clusters of berries have swung upside down on the slender branches of the elder, a sign they are ripe. Elderberry cordial is said to be good for the immune system. Sitting on the van step, I strip hundreds of berries into a pan, and throw the scarlet stalks (to which a few recalcitrant berries cling) a few feet away for the birds to pick at. I add water and sugar to the berries and simmer them, until the juice is viscous as blood ... then strain the cordial into bottles. The warm wad of flesh and pips left behind in the stained linen is shocking: solid and sanguine as a severed heart.

The last buds at the tip of the hollyhock spike. White campion and yarrow still flowering in the verges.

Sunday 5 September

The assassin was hoping to get the roof on the new building before winter. So far, only the fundamentals are in place: an ivory Buddha in the eaves, coins beneath the step.

'A bit like writing a book,' I commiserate. 'But we're getting there slowly.'

'Slowly is the fucking operative word.' He shows Sven and me a picture of the wood-burning stove he's ordered. 'Look at that. It's a work of art.'

The white dog licks my ankles.

'We just came down to steal stuff really,' I say.

'You haven't got a grill, or any cast-iron stove plate?' Sven pokes through the junk by the picnic table for something to raise the bed of my stove. 'We thought you might have some old shit lying around...'

'That is the definition of this place,' says the assassin. 'Around the corner, that's where shit gravitates, we'll go and have a look. Let's have some tea first. How's the CO situation?'

'Okay. It's around 10 ppm when I make coffee.'

'Fuck! It should read zero. Well, you're dealing with a vast unknown. When territory is unknown, you must encroach on it gradually, slowly building up pockets of familiarity. Otherwise it remains incomprehensible. The first elements you understand are stepping stones to see the whole. Help yourself to biscuits, guys.' He pops a hobnob in his mouth. 'Have you tried the chocolate ones? Very good.'

'Relationships between things are primary in this world, more important than the things themselves. Consider Benjamin Franklin, who used a kite to show that electricity and lightning were part of the same phenomenon. You have to understand the connections between everything. Controlling matter is not just a case of levers, as in *The Sorcerer's Apprentice*, but empathy.'

A robin watches us from the bare rafters. The assassin lays a crumb on his palm and holds out his hand. 'Here you are, little man. . .

'So, with the functions of your van, take the water heater for example, which is a true mystery to us all, we don't know whether it works off the gas or the electricity or both. And you have the batteries and the charger that may not charge. Yet in all this, I believe gas is the greatest unknown.' He looks very serious. 'Yes, gas is the unknown . . .'

The robin flies down for the crumb.

Benjamin Franklin's kite experiment with 'Electric Fire' was reported in the *Pennsylvania Gazette* on 19 October 1752 as follows:

> Make a small Cross of two light Strips of Cedar, the Arms so long as to reach to the four Corners of a large thin Silk Handkerchief when extended; tie the Corners of the Handkerchief to the Extremities of the Cross, so you have the Body of a Kite; which being properly accommodated with a Tail, Loop and String, will rise in the Air, like those made of Paper; but this being of Silk is fitter to bear the Wet and Wind of a Thunder Gust without tearing. To the Top of the upright Stick of the Cross is to be fixed a very sharp pointed Wire, rising a Foot or more above the Wood. To the End of the Twine, next the Hand, is to be tied a silk Ribbon, and where the Twine and the silk join, a Key may be fastened. This Kite is to be raised when a Thunder Gust

appears to be coming on, and the Person who holds the String must stand within a Door, or Window, or under some Cover, so that the Silk Ribbon may not be wet; and Care must be taken that the Twine does not touch the Frame of the Door or Window. As soon as any of the Thunder Clouds come over the Kite, the pointed Wire will draw the Electric Fire from them, and the Kite, with all the Twine, will be electrified, and the loose Filaments of the Twine will stand out every Way, and be attracted by an approaching Finger. And when the Rain has wet the Kite and Twine, so that it can conduct the Electric Fire freely, you will find it stream out plentifully from the Key on the Approach of your Knuckle. At this Key the Phial may be charged; and from Electric Fire thus obtained, Spirits may be kindled, and all the other Electric Experiments be perform'd, which are usually done by the Help of a rubbed Glass Globe or Tube; and thereby the Sameness of the Electric Matter with that of Lightning completely demonstrated.

Monday 6 September

First sunny day after weeks of grey weather. I throw the cushions outside to air.

Tuesday 7 September

Long before we met, Anna had cycled from Land's End to John o'Groats, but I never knew her get on a bike in the decade we spent together. In this city of bicycles, she preferred her car.

Now once a week she attends Wheels for All at the stadium used by Harlequin RFC beyond the ring road, close to the Cowley works. The 400-metre track has the same footprint as the university sports centre on the Iffley Road where Roger Bannister ran the four-minute mile in 1954, but here the triumphs are harder won.

One of the Wheels for All volunteers, a breezy guy called Bruce, buddies up with her. He adapts each bike and fits stabilisers where required. Nothing is impossible – he digs an endless supply of bike parts out of a shipping container by the stands. I film Anna doing circuits of the track on my phone. She rides a recumbent bike, then switches to an electric tricycle and a bicycle with stabilisers.

'I couldn't do that six months ago,' Anna says as we head back to the flat.

I squeeze her shoulder. 'You're the yellow jersey. I'm terribly proud of you.'

Wednesday 8 September

On the other side of the canal, the city is coming closer. A long-planned 'Northern Gateway' is under development. The existing carriageway is being widened, and the steady thump of construction joins the hum of traffic from the overpass. The grinding of heavy machinery. The green fields are now topsoil, rutted by caterpillar treads. Runoff forms a stagnant pool. The city council has identified a 'key strategic site' of 44 hectares, to 'position employment space for the knowledge economy'. The land is being cleared for 90,000 square metres of office space, and hundreds of new homes and shops. A floodlight illuminates the ridge, night and day.

'You have to understand,' says the assassin, when I grumble about the beeps and clanks in the early morning and late after dark. 'This is entirely a human-made landscape. The canal, obviously, was cut out from the ground, that's why they call it "the cut", but also the railway embankment has been raised up. Banked up. And the woods are in a sort of compromise position, between them. And those lakes, over beyond the tracks, indeed many of the lakes here, exist because topsoil and stone for the embankment had to be quarried from somewhere. All this is a construct: a stage set for trains and boats to move through. Don't think this greenery around us is any more natural than the canal and the rails either side.'

He tells me that even the railway was unwelcome once. The main works for Great Western were defeated here and went to Swindon, and construction on the railway was delayed until 1844. 'Very few people in Oxford wanted the railway. Some rascal built a house of brown paper on the proposed line of the track, and demanded substantial compensation for its removal. But everything must change. Did you know the village once had its own railway halt?'

Imagine flagging down a train from my van. 'What's the difference between a station and a halt?'

'Well, halts normally have no buildings or staff. They're a bit of a secret, the train won't normally stop there. A request stop.'

Although it was merely a halt, it *was* staffed, and during the First World War it became the first station to have a stationmistress, a woman called Margaret Elsden. Her brother was stationmaster of Birmingham's Snow Hill. And she later married Frank Buckingham, who became stationmaster at Oxford. A family profession. I wonder what thoughts passed through Margaret's mind, standing on the exposed siding, watching engines pull away – south and north – in the direction of her husband and brother. I wonder how she kept track of time.

Thursday 9 September

Sven's birthday.

We should do something to celebrate, I told Aislin last week. He's always helping us, and yet he won't allow himself any respite. He won't even take a night off. She calls the friendly head waiter and makes a special arrangement, and at nine o'clock we pile into the assassin's Land Rover and drive fast to Sven's in order to kidnap him, a job the assassin performs with practised cool, and bundle him into the vehicle. Where are we going? Sven asks crossly, dragging the pillowcase off his head. Oh, just Ali's kebab van, Aislin laughs and begins to sing *happy birthday*. The camaraderie in the vehicle is intoxicating, as we drive down the dark lane towards the river.

There has been a pub here at the weir for centuries. Walkers came once for *eel tea*, stewed eels washed down by unlimited cider cup, but these days the menu is fancier. We're at sea among the polished cutlery and heavy napkins and our spirits sink a little. I order a bottle of Muscadet for the table. The assassin demands venison meatballs.

'Sweetheart, we're only here for dessert,' says Aislin.

Sven is in a philosophical mood. He embarks on a homily: what might we do with the lives we've been given? 'Take Michael Faraday. Faraday encountered a world of science from which the working class was excluded. In the eighteenth century science was a gentlemen's sport. You needed to be independently wealthy to pursue experiments. You couldn't grow up in the backstreets of Liverpool like Faraday and just say, "Oh, I'll be a scientist." It didn't work like that. But he found a way through. His father apprenticed him to a bookseller, and he educated himself by reading all the books.

'Look what an innovative scientist he was, and he came from nothing. This is the inventor of electricity! He discovered the electromagnetic field!' Sven thumps the table and the cutlery bounces. 'They said to him at the time, "This electricity is all very well, Mister Faraday, but what will we do with it?" A bit like cryptocurrency at the moment. He was a visionary, ahead of his time. His research underpins all today's technology.'

'Do you think his brilliance came in part from being on the outside?' I ask.

'I'm talking like I'm an expert on Faraday. I'm not. But science is not just analysis. The best scientists are creative people. They examine the foundations of thought, and they come up with revolutionary ways of looking at things. Faraday was an experimental scientist. Like Mendel, the founding father of genetics, who was a monk, and very poor – yes, an outsider. Einstein too. Einstein kept a picture of Faraday on his study wall. Einstein could *not* get a job in science. Would you believe it! *Einstein*. He was too much of an oddball. He worked in the patent office in Switzerland, doing his scientific research as a hobby.'

'We know all these names,' I manage to interject, 'but there must have been other brilliant minds who just broke down under life's pressures, whose research never saw the light of day . . .'

'I put my hand up!'

'It's the same in the arts. You have to find a way of smashing through difficult circumstances . . . making your work *and* making sure it is seen.'

'Yes, and if you don't get support, you're toast. Look at all the wasted potential in the world. Where are Mendel's contemporaries? They're just sacks of bones and ashes now.'

'Mendel challenged the attitudes of his time,' says Aislin. 'In the Middle Ages people believed there were humours in the body: bile, blood, and so on. A hot temper was to do with bloods being warmed up. The humours were linked to the four elements: earth, air, fire and water. To be healthy, all the elements needed to be in balance. Even the environment, cold winds and so on could influence these humours. At the time that was the gold standard.'

Our *tarte Tatin* arrives, and meatballs and waffles for the assassin.

'I've seen the flack scientists get from the establishment when they question things. You can't persuade people,' Sven concludes. 'You have to leave it a generation. Twenty years later people see the sense of what you're saying and it's not polluted by jiggery-pokery and politics. Funding. Egos. Attitudes to women, to gay people. Rosalind Franklin took a whole bunch of shit. It was outrageous that she was left out of the Nobel Prize. Did I ever tell you about my moment of fame, when I showed Watson, of Watson and Crick, the way to the khazi?'

Friday 10 September

Thirteen swans on the river. I walk to the tiny limestone chapel at Binsey to play the harmonium. Between the hawthorn hedges the narrow lane is scattered with beech mast and squirrels scrabble in the branches overhead.

Electricity has never been installed at St Margaret's – the occasional services are still candlelit. I push open the heavy wooden door, and step into the cool chancel. I open the lid of the harmonium, and move aside the yellowed newspapers which cover the keys. My reflection shimmers in the cracked glass of the mirror. I pull out an ivory stop marked in gothic script *vox humana* and begin to treadle.

In one corner of the churchyard, almost hidden behind an ancient yew, is a deep well that has been a place of pilgrimage for centuries. The stone steps leading to the dark pool are worn down in the middle. This site is mentioned in *Alice in Wonderland*, where it becomes the surreal 'treacle well' that confuses the sleepy dormouse at the Mad Hatter's tea party before he is dunked in the teapot. Lewis Carroll would have known that 'treacle' was a medieval term for a healing fluid. I don't believe the well waters will be any more curative for me than treacle, but I am drawn to this contemplative place. I find the ghostly company of previous pilgrims comforting.

As I stand in the dank hollow – where a few white chrysanthemums have been left by someone not long before me – I consider the story that predates Carroll's. The origins of the holy spring. Frideswide, a Mercian noblewoman, used her wealth to found a monastery and took a vow of celibacy. Algar, the king of Leicester, was captivated by Frideswide and when she refused his marriage proposal he made several attempts to abduct her. His relentless pursuit drove her into the woods beside the Thames, where she hid among swineherds for several seasons, and joined them in their work. Algar searched for her in Oxford, but the town's citizens refused to tell him where she was. His persistence was punished by divine intervention: he was blinded by lightning. At this crisis Algar repented, and in a moment of compassion Frideswide prayed for the restoration of his sight. At her words water sprang from the earth.

Frideswide is the patron saint of Oxford. On her tomb in the cathedral, the small ledger slab is surrounded by a monumental forest carved from stone. It includes the first depiction of a sycamore tree in English art.

Saturday 11 September

Coloured dots sprayed onto tree trunks and saplings tagged with bright strips of cloth hint at long-term conservation projects. The many nesting boxes are numbered, as are the moth traps. The road from Wytham is surfaced for conservationists' vehicles, but I soon leave this reliable route behind and wander along winding bridleways and under dark holloways and begin to lose my sense of direction in the dripping forest. Every few acres, I pass an observation platform surreal as a Louise Bourgeois etching – a steel ladder ascends to a folding seat high in the trees.

Out of the mist loom the titanic silver beeches of Marley Fen. The peat in this rare wetland purifies the water that flows through it, and preserves infinitesimal pollen grains and particles of pollution, caught as they travel through the water cycle. An underground herringbone pipe system was installed here in the 1870s to collect the clean, naturally filtered water; this began to erode the peat and the environmental archive was exposed to the air. Contemporary interventions are more sensitive. Today, it looks as if the beeches have wilfully twirled their own twigs into spirals. These strange alchemical spheres have been woven from willow and hazel by human hands to represent the mysterious, microscopic elements in the peat. 'So much is unseen,' writes the creator of this art installation in the trees, Hermeet Gill. Across millennia I feel the damp breath of wild auroch on the back of my neck. The midnight shuffle of a badger echoes in the undergrowth, beneath my feet changing patterns of water flow.

Sunday 12 September

To Jacob's Inn to finish the blot poems and email them to the BBC. I enjoy the luxury of a table to arrange my drafts. The waiter brings black coffee without waiting for an order, and lets me sit for hours after it goes cold.

The headline story is the kidnap and murder of Sarah Everard in March, for which Met police officer Wayne Couzens is soon to stand trial. There are editorials discussing violence against women, and my social media feeds have turned to memorials, a stream of photographs of candles with the hashtag #SheWasJustWalkingHome.

Nights are drawing in. It's dark when I head for home at eight o'clock. Houseboat windows glimmer on the still water. Some boats are strung with fairy lights and, as if reflected through gauze, I glimpse an occasional star in the muggy sky. Everyone is wary. I bump into the assassin who is making repairs to his butty with a head torch on. He leaps as I brush past.

'Hello,' I say.

'Fucking hell, I thought you were a skelm,' he says.

He asks what I do for self-defence, and offers me some illegal gear from his armoury. The spy novelist Len Deighton described Berlin as 'the only city in the world where you were safer in the dark'. Here, blending into the shadows on the towpath where I know the outline of every tree, I feel safer than I have in many brightly lit rooms, although I know I should be prepared for skelms.

'What you really want', the assassin says, 'is a massive torch. Light stuns – but it causes no harm, and leaves no marks. If you encounter any trouble, switch a light on suddenly and you'll completely disarm any opponent. And while you're in the dark, you have the upper hand. As you – uh – just saw. Hang on, I've got a spare somewhere.'

I walk back to the van, keeping one hand in my coat pocket on the reassuringly heavy 'Big Larry' Pro Torch.

Monday 13 September

Tuesday 14 September

Yesterday I took some books to my shipping container. When I opened the door there was a musty smell. Rainwater had found a hole in the rusting roof, and run down the inside walls or travelled along the ceiling. It had dripped down onto the cardboard boxes and soaked through into my books. The first box I opened contained catalogues on sculpture and stage design, exhibitions I'd reviewed and knew intimately, the paper swollen and runkled. Books inscribed by artists as gifts during times of collaboration, the ink now bleeding into the paper and the messages illegible. Boxes of poetry chewed into confetti by mice or consumed by snails. Memories of all the places I've been, all the people I've worked with. Journals I've edited, love letters, bank statements, draft manuscripts for books not yet complete. I open more and more boxes, desperate to find some things that are unharmed. But as I move towards the far end of the container, closer to the hole through which daylight gleams, the boxes become more waterlogged and the damage more extreme. I hold out hope that the books at the very back, which are most valuable to me, might have been saved. Books I made myself over the last decade, letterpress printed and hand-bound. But when I reach them, the archival-grade tissue paper in which they are wrapped peels away, and beneath it the delicate papers are already discoloured by insidious threads of mould.

I slump on the container sill. *A shock is good for your heart.* I know that worldly goods are nothing, compared to health. The poet Elizabeth Bishop would say the art of losing isn't hard to master. I don't believe I'm even upset over the loss of my books, not really. I'm just exhausted by relentless disaster. *I guess it never ends.* Each episode beats me further into the silt. I don't want to be in this story any more. Other writers appear on Zoom framed by sophisticated bookshelves. What would an audience think of the chaos behind me now?

Sven did say I had too much junk, I think, as my sobs subside. I pull out my phone and dial his number. Controlling my voice as well as I can, I say, 'Do you feel like driving to the tip?'

'Jesus! I'm going to take you back to the pet shop. I want an easier pet.'

Wednesday 15 September

Rain. A tiny snail crawls over the window, and from inside I can watch its pale foot undulating.

The van has darkened with algae and soot. Sand hill snails creep through the grime, heading for shelter in window frames and under the hitch head. Zigzag trails squiggle like the intricate sutures of the skull or the frills of foam left by an outgoing tide. They weave their heads from side to side as their radula scrape up the algae and stuff it into their mouths, hence the wobbly track. Their appetites are visible on the posters for the missing man too, which are still pinned up on the Elsan station and at intervals along the towpath. The snails have begun to chew their way through the paper, by this unsettled journey consuming the last evidence of his disappearance.

Anna has bought a primrose-yellow bicycle with stabilisers.

Thursday 16 September

The pre-op nurse called this morning. We spend thirty minutes on the phone, during which she fires a series of questions at me. Have you ever had a stroke? Have you ever had a heart attack? Do you have a heart murmur? How many pillows do you like to sleep on? How wide can you open your mouth – can you insert your fingers between your teeth to check please? Do you have reflux? What is your preferred name?

I mention the CO episode.

She is silent for a moment. That's clearly not on her list. 'You're already down as a high-risk patient. I'm going to request another blood test. I'm concerned about some of your readings. Can you come in today?'

My body, now it is being read with such care by consultants, seems to be shouting to express all the inconsistencies I have long been ignorant of. What I hoped was a discrete issue that would be removed or resolved by surgery becomes merely one aspect of a damaged organism that must be healthy enough to have surgery in the first place, a whole system that is under a discussion and analysis. There are infinitesimal interconnections and influences in this ecology I had never dreamed existed. I lie in bed, my hands resting on my belly, wondering about the narrative my body is drafting that I cannot yet read. Beneath my skin, a trapped and mutinous satellite thrums. Recalling Robert Hooke's study of objects that were not visible to the naked eye, I wonder whether this *shelly mound* might contain 'some kind of Mudd or Clay, or *petrifying* Water, or some other substance, which in tract of time has been settled together and hardned'. Will the imminent excavation and analysis of this chalk egg cure seasickness or lead me on a new journey? Medical letters arrive but they are really for doctors' eyes, and the fact I see them feels like a courtesy. The doctors' language is not my language. I'm curious. But I want only simple answers, and I'm content to leave the complex method to others. I cling onto the fact that the consultant calls me 'this pleasant forty-three-year-old woman' as if pleasantness might mitigate all other conditions. When the nurse asks if I have any questions, I say *no*.

As if my mission is not really the hospital, I go via the library in Summertown, and return *Food for Free*. In the sculpture garden a quotation from a poem by Coleridge is carved into the patio slabs: *Friendship is a sheltering tree.*

Friday 17 September

Misty morning. The cobwebs between the spikes on the gate are trimmed with dew: a confluence of nature and architecture, delicacy and defence. But gossamer is not as delicate as it seems. Spider silk is less dense than steel, yet weight for weight, it is stronger and tougher than steel.

I stuff a few mint leaves in a pot for tea. I am on tenterhooks. Every day I expect an ominous call from Neurology. Or there will be a blood test. I grow familiar with the personality of the different phone lines. The hospital plays a tinkling Chopin sequence that can be interrupted any second when the receptionist releases the hold button. The doctor's surgery has pop anthems, upbeat reggae, *you are number four in the queue.* Today there's a new option relayed by the automated message. *If you are calling about the loss of Dr Amery . . .* Holy shit. Even my doctor has died.

Meanwhile, it seems as if everyone is travelling again. The water level in the canal is low. A rush of pleasure trippers passes through the locks, making the most of the end of the season. Restrictions lift one after another, as Covid vaccines are rolled out. The international traffic-light system will soon be simplified, the 'amber' designation scrapped in favour of a single 'red' list. People are enjoying late holidays abroad, glorious days of sunshine in 'green' zones. The woods are beautiful, but I feel trapped.

An email from the artist Michèle Noach. She's organising her festival in Vadsø in Arctic Norway next spring – can I participate? My response is febrile, and perhaps even unprofessional – I explain I can't commit due to health issues. She replies swiftly, telling me she recently had major surgery on her eyes. 'In the midst of ill health things seem so far away, usual life remote and impossible,' she writes kindly. 'But then it improves by degree, if different, and we delight in any return to our old self. I am left with partial double vision, a strange hex for an artist, but glad to be able to see at all.' She promises to keep the departure gates open for me until the spring.

Saturday 18 September

I'm reading, when there's a knock at the door of the van.

'NANCY!' says Katie. 'I came to visit you.'

'That's nice,' I say, deep in *Gilgamesh*.

'Can I come in?'

'Does your mum know you're here?'

'Yes, we made a stone for you. Here.' She holds out a flat stone, the kind that would skim for miles if we were playing ducks and drakes.

'Gosh, you've painted it beautifully. Look at those pink and gold spots.' It's covered with hallucinogenic whirling patterns in glittery nail lacquer.

'I did the spots all by myself. My mum helped varnish it.'

'Thank you, it's a real treasure. I'm going to put it next to my other stone. Look.' I show her the thunderstone, which pales next to the bright artifice of Katie's gift.

'Oh, it's broken,' she says sadly.

'Well, yes. Some bits have broken off. Got lost and left in other places. It's very old, you see. But this is its shape now.'

She promises to come back and help me with the garden, soon. 'I can offer you some tips,' she says.

Sunday 19 September

I take a bus into the city centre. I've been grubbing around at the canal far too long. I find that the meadow has moved to the metropolis. In the middle of Broad Street, where the Protestant Martyrs were burned at the stake in the sixteenth century, five wooden planters, each the size of a parking bay, sustain a jaded crop of yarrow,

common ragwort, and sweet william. A sign reads: DO NOT WALK
ON THE MEADOW. A hopscotch has been painted neatly on the
tarmac, not far from the cross of granite setts which marks the exact
spot of the martyrdom. I almost expect to see a similar sign: DO NOT
JUMP ON THE HOPSCOTCH. Two women sit on benches outside
the mock-Tudor shopfronts, safely distanced, while a child toddles
between them.

There are no butterflies jizzing here, none of the tall grasses that
give the common its whispering magic. It is a costly parody installed
by a city council to distract from housing developments elsewhere.
One feature of lockdown for Anna and me was the increasingly
inventive (and fatalistic) hand-painted protest signs along the lane
that we walked daily, our pace so slow that I got to know every leaf
of the hedgerows. Here, on the edge of the flood plain, a patchwork
of small fields provided a wildlife corridor to nature reserves along
the Thames. A protest video is put up on YouTube with music from
Peggy Seeger, a folk singer who happens to live just around the corner. It remains online after the fields are levelled and the badger sett
is demolished by heavy machinery.

I go to look at the fossilised sea urchin in the Pitt Rivers Museum,
found in Sussex in 1911: the label reads, 'Shepherd's Crown placed
on window ledge outside to keep the Devil out.'

An ambulance is parked at the lift bridge with its back doors open.
Unusual to see any vehicles here, other than the assassin's Land Rover.
Out the corner of my eye I see movement, something approaching
along the towpath, not a bike nor a wheelbarrow. A gurney is being

ushered along, slowly, flanked by paramedics. They cross the bridge *clunk* and the burden is lifted inside the vehicle.

Monday 20 September

Message from the assassin:

> Jack is no longer with us.

But he is, I'm sure of it.

Tuesday 21 September

Up at four this morning reading the proof copy of Hannah Bourne-Taylor's book *Fledgling*. Out of the darkness comes rain and out of the rain comes birdsong. Slow, heavy drops on the skylight, and when the light returns, individual leaves bow and spring up again, bobbing and winking in the woods. The green takes on the pallor of the rain's grey veil. The chiffchaff is quiet. Rain streaks down the window. It patters on the roof, on the puddles forming on the path. Slow then speeding up again, like corn popping in a pan. After living with vocal silence I've become more receptive to sounds of all kinds. Now I listen to my surroundings as avidly as during lockdown I listened to Anna, hoping to grasp her meaning.

Wednesday 22 September

Equinox. The beginning of Autumn. Aislin gives me two pairs of warm 'caravan socks' she has knitted from grey alpaca wool.

Thursday 23 September

Veronica approaches the gate carrying a stack of wooden frames. In the misty woods, her white smock and veil are good camouflage. The bees have succumbed to wax moth, she tells me. This moth lays its eggs in the hive and when they hatch, the larvae burrow through the comb, lining their tunnels with silken thread, and gorging themselves on wax. Veronica shows me the matted mass of silk and frass on the dark comb, the aftermath of the larvae party.

'The queen left,' she says, 'so the colony was more vulnerable. Disease swept in.'

The larvae have damaged the cells in which honey is stored, and also the brood comb, which cradled the pupae of the bees.

'What can you do?' I ask.

'Just start again next year,' she says, wearily. 'Hope for a new colony to come.'

Who do you tell about a death, when all the bees have died?

Friday 24 September

The invention of the moving image was aided by a scientific treatise on how wheels go round. 'A curious optical deception takes place when a carriage wheel, rolling along the ground, is viewed through the intervals of a series of vertical bars, such as those of a palisade.' Pierre Roget watched the wheels and the bars, the wheels and the bars. His *Explanation of an optical deception in the appearance of the spokes of a wheel* was published on New Year's Day, 1825. In time others read of this *curious deception* and the idea of moving images, the idea of an image that would spin around a drum occurred to them. The zoetrope, the 'wheel of life', was invented in 1866, a parlour game – an animation device that produced the illusion of motion through a sequence of drawings. The images were placed within, and the drum spun, and the motionless came to life. Discrete phases of motion blurred into one story, the past was animate for anyone peeping through – and then the first film reels began to turn. Those early films were silent, and anyway, too short to merit words.

Already Roget had moved on, had become a collector of words, binding the most similar into small groups (a dictionary jumbled into themes) with an alphabetical index, published in 1852. He ordered the words around classes like spokes of a wheel. *Class I: Words expressing Abstract Relations: Existence, Relation, Quantity, Order, Number, Time, Change, Causation*. A physician who never saw a film, a concrete poet who never knew his synonyms would circle the world piled in squat columns of varying heights, black on white. *Class IV: Words Expressing Motion: Motion, Quiescence, Traveller, Transference, Vehicle, Direction, Deviation* ... I flick through the codex, chasing the right word.

In a linear journey there are always new things to see. Such a journey is made only one way, as a tourist might travel from one end of an island to another, with no need to ever turn back. By contrast, cycling around a velodrome is a distraction from onward purpose. The loop suggests that by circuitous action we can, counter-intuitively, live with more intensity by staying in one place. I find it consoling to watch Anna on the bicycle's steel frame circle the Harlequin track over and over again like a charm against endings – Tears for Fears' 'Everybody Wants to Rule the World' playing over the stadium speakers, the men in the video dancing in front of petrol pumps – even though a loop is a journey that ends before it has begun. Watching Anna, I drift into a reverie on recovery. I see how much she has accomplished, with excruciating persistence, in the last two years. I remember that Roget was not only a physician and the inventor of the thesaurus but also a chess connoisseur. He designed a portable chessboard, and solved the general open Knight's tour problem by making repetitive moves within space, moving his pieces against those of a partner, until finally the Knight's progress through every square on the board was no longer foiled. Then he composed other problems, so there were always more problems to solve.

Saturday 25 September

Visit the *Roots and Seeds* exhibition at the Bodleian Library. One wall in the gallery is occupied by a xylarium, or library of wood. The polished timber samples look uncannily like leather spines, but these books do not require opening – the significance is in the colour, the grain, the weight. I remember John Cage's experimental composition for handbells, jotted down on a plywood board in the 1960s, in which the musical notation follows the grain structure of the wood. Afterwards, to Anna's for dinner: char sui pork served with lightly steamed pak choi. She sprinkles elegantly julienned spring onions over the rice. It's delicious.

Later I'm surprised to find an email in my inbox. The subject line: 'what would I miss'. Emails are rare between us now. Speech-to-text software enables vital messages, but epic communications are a thing of the past. *Everything takes so much time.*

The email contains a poem Tadeusz Różewicz wrote for Wisława. There's no signature, no other words.

what would I miss

Wisława's smile
when she says goodnight
or good morning

or when she says nothing

when she closes the door behind me
or opens it
after a long journey
or upon my return
from a land far off from her
when I was constructing a poem

what would I miss

the quiet between our faces
And words left
unspoken
because what is sacred
among human beings
constantly seeks
expression

what would I miss

my whole life
and something else
grand wonderful
beyond words
beyond body

Sunday 26 September

Soon it will be Apple Day. In the community orchard by the Thames the fruit is ripening. Plums drop onto the damp earth. Yellow apples decay under the trees. There are hundreds of species here, the taxonomy of each inscribed on a slim metal tag hung on the craggy branches. At the heart of the orchard is a medlar tree grafted onto a quince rootstock. The Royal Medlar Quince is a kaleidoscope of colours – green, yellow, brown and blood red – and still a few star-shaped flowers on the tips of the tangled branches. Medlars are late to fruit. In folk medicine the leaves, bark, fruits and wood were all used to treat digestive and menstrual complaints. The tough round fruits with their knotted, obscene calyx ripen only when frosts start, and are picked and eaten when bletted (going soft) in midwinter. During the Middle Ages it was a source of sugar in a time of dearth, and writers revered the symbolism of a fruit that is rotten before it is ripe.

Monday 27 September

Nights are drawing in. The undergrowth and brambles have died back, replaced by tufts of old man's beard. The busy life of the towpath feels closer. I overhear the conversations of people passing by. The world seemed so distant all summer, but it was only a temporary screen of leaves.

Everyone is preparing for winter. I shake flies from mesh windows, drain the water tank. Dusty the coalman comes on his barge from Stoke Bruerne in the Midlands, bringing kilo bags of FireGold, WinterBlaze, Smokeless Ovals and Anthracite Hard Nuts for the boaters' stoves and a butane cylinder for my van.

The sweep is brushing *Rigmarole*'s chimney. Logs are already neatly stacked on Prerona's deck.

The towpath is slippery with leaves. John Evelyn writes:

> The sycomor, or wild fig-tree, (falsly so called) is one of the maples, and is much more in reputation for its shade than it deserves; for the honey-dew leaves, which fall early (like those of the ash) turn to mucilage and noxious insects, and putrifie with the first moisture of the season; so as they contaminate and mar our walks; and are therefore by my consent, to be banish'd from all curious gardens and avenues.

Ariel crouches on *Nordica*'s roof, scrubbing away the grime of summer and putrified leaves.

'Alright?' I say. 'I haven't seen you around.'

She's been across Sweden on her motorbike. 'Good to be back in my tumblehome. Are you having fun in the van?'

I tell her everything. 'It's not been exactly *fun*.'

'Do you need anything? How are you getting to hospital?'

'I'm not sure. I have to isolate, so I can't take the bus.'

'Want me to give you a lift?'

Tuesday 28 September

News of petrol shortages. Tankers cannot deliver fuel because of the scarcity of qualified drivers. The pumps are empty. There are reports of fights breaking out at petrol stations, as panicking motorists queue to fill their tanks. Sven uses up his precious fuel to drive out beyond the ring road, and passes one closed petrol station after another, the entrances blocked off with bollards or chains. Should he carry on, or turn back?

A friend sends me a book of pictures. John Cage created visual as well as musical compositions. In these artworks too, the paper is scored with silence. For some drawings he used smoke, in others, stones. Kathan Brown, director of Crown Point Press in California, persuaded the composer to visit each year to work on a new sequence; she describes how when the printers were entangled in a technical problem Cage 'objected to our problem's being a problem'. He would say: 'We must be free of such concerns!' Cage persisted through difficulties, the difficulties became the work: 'Act in accordance with obstacles,' he wrote.

As the sun is setting I walk to the ruins at Godstow, and sit by the river as the light fades. The trees on the crest of the hill are spare silhouettes. The last minutes of the day feel immense. I take out my phone and, as a charm against mischance, book a train ticket to Brussels on a date in November.

Wednesday 29 September

Heatwave. A tubby red woodpecker drums in the willow, while I'm speaking to a friend on the phone.

Thursday 30 September

A faint light beyond the trees at 6 a.m. I am awake long before the alarm. I make my bed and tidy the caravan. Bid it a silent farewell. The van might seem scruffy to others: disordered bookshelves, a door that doesn't really shut, temperamental hot water, but it's the most congenial home I've ever known. I consider pocketing the thunderstone and taking it with me to hospital. But I leave it, and step out of the van resolving to return, as soon as I can.

Leaves are turning the potholes into golden pools. The effusive blossom of late spring is long gone. At the end of the lane, a cheerful silhouette: Ariel is waiting on her motorbike. Out of the mist the first bird calls, the boldest and bravest of the dawn chorus. Ariel hands me a helmet, and all other sounds are lost as she starts the engine.

The first stage of hospitalisation: a paper identity bracelet on each of my wrists. I let myself be defined by QR codes and a medical number, I abandon myself to the process. I sign all the forms. A canula is inserted in the back of my hand. My bed is by the window, which is open a crack because of the heatwave, and in the world beyond I can see a sliver of pavement, and a robin picking up crumbs.

My bed is by the window, which is open a crack because of the heatwave, and the world outside is dark. Somebody says my name. The nurses call me *lovely* and *darling* as they take my blood pressure every hour. *That's very good, darling. Would you like some more pain relief?*

There is the robin again. The sighing cuffs are removed from my legs. Dr Li pads around the blue curtain, and shows me images taken by the laparoscope, her scalpel probing deep in my abdomen.

I do my groggy best to express my gratitude. The procedure was quite straightforward, she smiles. You will have scar tissue. Peel it away, she says, it's good to keep refreshing the wound. Histology will be carried out by the lab and I'll inform you myself if there is any pathology. Meanwhile, please don't worry. No swimming and no sex for two months. The nurse tells me you are living in a caravan? That must be wonderful.

When the lights dim again I am determined to walk around the ward. If I can walk, then I can go home. Around midnight I roll off the bed and shuffle down the corridor. I am a dopey ghost in my paper mask, white surgical stockings and hospital gown. A glass door is ajar to let in the breeze. I slide it open further, and with a cautious glance back at the nurses' station I step gingerly into the dark courtyard. I'm surprised my escape doesn't trigger an alarm.

Cool air on my skin. Familiar ironwork flowers and scorched palms. I lower myself onto a bench in the neglected garden, among shadowy clumps of dwarf yew and laurel; at my feet, a profuse wild strawberry, the berries overlooked.

Brightly lit windows rise on all sides of this cloister, disrupting my night vision. Faintly, a baby's cry. Of course – above gynaecology, maternity. An ambulance siren passes and stalls. I raise my eyes higher, to the fifth floor of the gargantuan block, the window I stared out of two years ago. I wonder who is sitting there now.

I am sitting there. Time compresses like an accordion. The slow tender note it plays is a blessing I send to my former self.

I can see one bright star. My eyes will find others, if I stay a while. I don't feel any rush to move. For how long Anna and I have circled this hospital on a hill. We found ourselves in the same strata of time and for a while we shared a life, our hours; a small home, barely even a room; a lockdown; then just a city; and the drift will carry us further. A poet might write of one loss as a simile for another, but there is no need to force anything. A generative organ is cut away. A working limb grows numb. Heads break, hearts break. We learn to live with paralysis, pathology. Thunder strikes and forges a new star on a stone. The urchin nestles deeper in the silt. Seas rise and ice retreats, and a woman finds a fossil in the rubble and places it in her pocket.

It is easy enough to say, for example, that such and such a day was rainy in the morning but fine in the afternoon, that there was a pine tree at such and such a place, or that the name of a river at a certain place was such-and-such, for these things are what everybody says in their diaries, although in fact they are not worth mentioning unless there are fresh and arresting elements in them. The reader will find in my diary a random collection of what I have seen on the road, views somehow remaining in my heart … I jotted down these records with the hope that they might provoke pleasant conversations among my readers and that they might be of some use to those who would travel the same way.

MATSUO BASHŌ,
'RECORDS OF A TRAVEL-WORN SATCHEL'

ACKNOWLEDGEMENTS

The story of this caravan was made possible by collaborative daring and dreaming.

Henry David Thoreau boasted in *Walden* that he needed only three chairs: 'one for solitude, two for friendship, three for society'. Likewise, my caravan had relatively few visitors due to the pandemic, but I was never short of virtual company. I was fortunate to have the safety net (sometimes more of an emerald hammock) of friends and colleagues, in particular Astrid Alben, John Bently, Kaddy Benyon, Julia Bird, Sarah Bodman, Emily Brett, Angela Butler, Isabel Brittain, Ken Campbell, Claudia Casanova, J. R. Carpenter, Horatio Clare, Jo Clement, Patrick and Janet Cooper, Jeremy Dixon, Kerri ní Dochartaigh, Nick Drake, Will Eaves, Kitty Evans, Nora Gomringer, Sally Huband, Nasim Marie Jafry, Kirsten Jüdt, Ralph Kiggell, Alicia Kopf, Alexandra Loske, Yvonne Love, Morag McCracken, Leonard and Jean McDermid, Helen Mitchell, Graham Moss, Judith Palmer, Linda Parr, Joanna Pocock, Katie and Lynden Potter, Dan Richards, Gabrielle Russomagno, Martí Salas, Sarah Thomas, Matthew Teller, and Ruth Valentine. My especial thanks to Kirsten Norrie and Alexis Thompson. The final draft of the manuscript was completed in a room overlooking the River North Esk at Hawthornden Castle in Scotland; it was a great privilege to borrow this desk, and enjoy the vital companionship of Alta Ifland, Sam Kuhn, Madame Nielsen, Guy Stagg, and Alice White, under the patient aegis of Hamish Robinson.

This book describes recent events, but it is also the tale of my engagement with the city of Oxford over two decades. Like the ecology of woodland and lakes, canal and meadow, my research draws on the knowledge of many individuals: boat dwellers, health professionals, gardeners, and those artists and assassins who would doubtless prefer to slip sideways away from any labels. I am grateful to everyone who interrupted their work, carpentry, cleaning, dreaming, and gardening to talk to me. To protect people's privacy, some names (where known) have been changed.

These journals have been edited for the benefit of readers since the summer's events diminished my capacity, but they keep to the essence of my original notebooks. Extracts were published in *Dark Mountain*, *Linseed Journal* and *The Clearing*; my thanks to respective editors Charlotte Du Cann, Louise Long and Jon Woolcott for giving these words a home.

The presence of the following people coloured the hours of this summer and my story would be incomplete without them.

Anna Zvegintzov, for telling me to bugger off and then letting me come back from time to time to do my laundry, and with characteristic grace and generosity allowing me to publish these notes about our lives together. I hope one day to read her side of the story. 'Sven' for his limitless imagination and his impatience to solve all the problems life presents, even when that problem is a poet; for being the mature and sensible Emerson to my scruffy and idealistic Thoreau. Phil and Emma, Usher and Thornley for their welcome. Sue (and Tony) Maufe, and Imi Maufe, for showing me that it is possible to live well and work well in a small space, and even have fun. I am indebted to the artist Mette-Sofie D. Ambeck, who introduced me to thunderstones.

My gratitude to the team at Elliott and Thompson for their faith in this book, and to Sarah Rigby – the most clear-sighted and compassionate of editors. And (always) Kirsty McLachlan, my agent.

I remember with awe the skill and professionalism of the doctors and staff of the John Radcliffe Hospital and the Churchill Hospital in Oxford who, within the space of two years and each side of a lockdown, saved both Anna's life and mine, and the Nuffield Orthopaedic Hospital where Anna began her recovery.

With special gratitude to Dr Yvonne Nsiah and in memory of Dr Justin Amery.

NOTES

all these and most other kinds – Robert Hooke: *Micrographia; or, Some Physiological Descriptions of Minute Bodies Made by Magnifying Glasses, with Observations and Inquiries Thereupon* (The Royal Society, 1665), via the Royal Society online library, royalsociety.org

Lockdown

All day, all night – Virginia Woolf's essay 'On Being Ill' is collected in *The Moment and Other Essays* (Hogarth Press, 1947).

this curious sense of being pulled – Denise Riley, *Time Lived, Without Its Flow* (Picador, 2019)

Returning to Earth – Buzz Aldrin, interview by Scholastic students, 17 November 1998, at http://teacher.scholastic.com/space/apollo11/interview.htm

THUNDER over THUNDER. *Poplar fluff* – I use the I Ching app generated by Brian Fitzgerald, at ichingappofchanges.com, and all quotations in the text are from this source.

June

'Because a thing is going strong now' – The epigraph and quotations throughout the book from E. M. Forster's *Howards End* use the 2000 Penguin Classics edition with introduction and notes by David Lodge.

'A poet is a pirate,' he says often – Jean Daive, *Under the Dome: Walks with Paul Celan*, translated by Rosemarie Waldrop (City Lights, 2020)

The earth shows up those of value – John Berger, *Into Their Labours: Pig Earth* (Granta, 1992) on a saying quoted by Jean Pierre Vernant in *Mythe et Pensée Chez le Grecs*; subsequent quotations from *Into Their Labours* are taken from this edition.

I loved you, so I drew these tides – T. E. Lawrence, 'To S.A.'; the dedication to *Seven Pillars of Wisdom* (Cape, 1935)

by the vulgar at least – quoted by Ken McNamara in *Dragon's Teeth and Thunderstones: The Quest for the Meaning of Fossils* (Reaktion, 2020); Robert Plot was the first keeper of the Ashmolean Museum

flames glided in the river – the Little Free Library copy of Joseph Conrad's *Heart of Darkness* was published by Penguin in 1973; all subsequent quotations are taken from this edition

using the wrong words – Anne Carson used London Underground stops and signs, and Bertolt Brecht's FBI file, as well as her microwave manual in 'A Fragment of Ibykos Translated Six Ways', *London Review of Books*, Vol. 34 No. 21, 8 November 2012

Coffee too has its marvels – this, and other extracts from John Muir throughout the text, are taken from his journal *My First Summer in the Sierra* (Canongate, 1988) poems about blots – the poems were published in *Uneasy Pieces* (Guillemot Press, 2022)

forms without lines – Cozens explains the technique in detail in *A New Method of Assisting the Invention in Drawing Original Compositions of Landscape* (1786)

jumble of things – Leonardo da Vinci, *Treatise on Painting* (the English edition of 1877, translated by John Francis Rigaud)

A tiny wren perched – John Fowles, *The French Lieutenant's Woman* (Triad/Granada, 1981)

subduing Acrid humours of the stomach – John Woodward, *An Attempt towards a Natural History of the Fossils of England* (London, 1729), quoted by Ken McNamara in *Dragon's Teeth and Thunderstones*, op. cit.

on the kankodori and *sabihisha* – R. H. Blyth, *Haiku: Volume 3, Summer–Autumn* (Hokuseido Press, 1984)

A poor body might in an hour's space – John Evelyn, *Sylva, or A Discourse of Forest-Trees and the Propagation of Timber* (1664)

temporary home – Elizabeth Jennings, 'Advice to Myself and Other Poets' in Elizabeth Jennings Papers, Georgetown University, quoted in the epilogue to Dana Greene, *Elizabeth Jennings: The Inward War* (Oxford, 2018)

fulcrum – Elizabeth Jennings, 'Drying Up', ibid.

ramshackle – Greene, op. cit.

'On the Move Again' – Elizabeth Jennings, in Elizabeth Jennings Papers, Georgetown University, op. cit.

One mourns when one accepts – Judith Butler, *Precarious Life: The Powers of Mourning and Violence* (Verso, 2006)

Global landscapes today are strewn with ruin – Anna Lowenhaupt Tsing, *The Mushroom at the End of the World: On the Possibility of Life in Capitalist Ruins* (Princeton University Press, 2015)

In May, I sing night and day – traditional

Baucis and Philemon – in Ovid, *Metamorphosis*, viii

railway spine – John Eric Erichsen, *On Railway and Other Injuries of the Nervous System* (Philadelphia, 1867)

The first trees were ferns – Anselm Kiefer and Michael Auping, *Anselm Kiefer: Heaven and Earth* (Museum of Modern Art of Fort Worth, 2005); *Secret of the Ferns / Geheimnis der Farne* was first exhibited at Kiefer's retrospective at the Grand Palais, Paris in 2007; on mourning in Kiefer, I am indebted to Yota Batsaki's essay 'The Apocalyptic Herbarium: Mourning and Transformation in Anselm Kiefer's *Secret of the Ferns*' in *Environmental Humanities* 13:2 (November 2021)

mauve nostalgia – Derek Jarman, *Smiling in Slow Motion: Journals 1991–1994* (Vintage, 2018)

Nothing in English can capture – Anne Carson, *NOX* (New Directions, 2010)

You can read in the space – Annie Dillard, *The Writing Life* (Harper Collins, 2013)

Two fingers of his left hand – John Berger, *Into Their Labours: Once in Europa* (Granta, 1992)

July

And still, in the beautiful City – Alfred Noyes, 'Oxford Revisited', in *The Golden Hynde: And Other Poems* (Macmillan, 1914)

slap in the middle – Jan Morris, *Oxford* (Oxford University Press, 1978)

mousey-smelling – Robert Graves, *The White Goddess* (Faber and Faber, 1999)

Boar's Hill – Evelyn Waugh, *Brideshead Revisited* (Penguin Classics, 2020)

a neighbour rented us – Robert Graves, *Goodbye to All That* (Penguin Modern Classics, 2000)

as I can breathe and drum – Günter Grass, *The Tin Drum*, translated by Breon Mitchell (Houghton Mifflin Harcourt, 2009)

though I may keep a leafy twig – Henry David Thoreau, *The Journal 1837–1861* (NYRB Books 2009); subsequent quotations from Thoreau's journals are from this edition

What are you struggling for? – Emily Carr, *Hundreds and Thousands: The Journals of Emily Carr* (Clarke, Irwin & Co., 1966)

Yea, the sparrow hath found her a house – Psalm 84:3, American Standard Version

So I prophesied as I was commanded – Ezekiel 37:7–10, King James Version

What to do in this old and untimely body? – Kate Briggs, *This Little Art* (Fitzcarraldo Editions, 2017)

The most enlightening moments of my life – Agnes Martin, *With My Back to the World* (New Deal Films, 2002) at https://ubu.com/film/martin_wind.html

We were coming down the street – Oscar Wilde, 'Art and the Handicraftsman' in *Essays and Lectures* (Methuen, 1908)

so undramatic, so gentle – Jan Morris, *Oxford* (Oxford University Press, 1978)

Some shape of beauty – John Keats, *Endymion*, Book I, lines 12–13, at https://poets.org/poem/endymion-book-i-thing-beauty-joy-ever

eye lashes – Keats in a letter to J. H. Reynolds on 21 September 1817, in Suzie Grogan, *John Keats: Poetry, Life and Landscape* (Pen & Sword, 2021)

Pipe – Matt Gaw, *The Pull of the River* (Elliott & Thompson, 2018)

Stevenson's own boat – see Robert Louis Stevenson's *An Inland Voyage* (first published 1878) for an account of this voyage

another far more reclusive type of urchin – Ken McNamara, *Dragon's Teeth and Thunderstones: The Quest for the Meaning of Fossils*, op. cit.

Very seductive are the first steps – Emerson in his Journal, August 1848, *The Complete Works of Ralph Waldo Emerson* (Houghton, Mifflin and Company, 1904)

butterflies on the teasels – Derek Jarman, *Modern Nature* (Vintage, 1992)

August

Dorthe Nors, excerpt from 'Days' from *So Much for That Winter: Novellas* (Graywolf Press, 2016), translated from the Danish by Misha Hoekstra.

how astonishing, when the lights of health go down, the undiscovered countries – Virginia Woolf, 'On Being Ill', op. cit.

suspicion of rain – Jarman, *Modern Nature*, op. cit.

The lowest berry – Richard Mabey, *Food for Free* (HarperCollins, 2012)

There is nothing more evocative – Jan Morris, *Trieste and the Meaning of Nowhere* (Faber & Faber, 2002)

they are afraid of not being carried – Christos Galanis, 'Water Spiders, Settlers and Other Surface Dwellers: A Conversation with Stephen Jenkinson', in *Dark Mountain 19* (spring 2021)

Civilisation, it seems to me – William Morris, *News from Nowhere* (Oxford University Press, 2003)

misery – William Morris, in speeches such as 'Art and Democracy', 1883, which marked his public outing as a socialist the city was poorer than Oldham – Michael Noble et al., *Changing Patterns of Income and Wealth in Oxford and Oldham* (University of Oxford Department of Applied Social Studies and Social Research, 1994)

terminus – Beatrix Campbell, *Goliath: Britain's Dangerous Places* (Methuen, 1993)

By the 1990s, many in Blackbird Leys were unemployed – 'There were 30,000 people employed in manufacturing in Oxford (mostly male) in the 1970s, by 1990 that figure had declined to 5,000,' ibid.

To live as we choose – Campbell, op. cit.

I can ramble around here – Tove Jansson, letter to Eva Konikoff, 19 July 1946, in *Tove Jansson: Letters from Tove*, edited by Boel Westin and Helen Svensson, translated by Sarah Death (Sort Of Books, 2019)

We did many foolish things – Tove Jansson, 'Notes from an Island' ('Anteckningar från en ö')

strokes of havoc – Gerard Manley Hopkins, 'Binsey Poplars', at Poetry Foundation, https://www.poetryfoundation.org/poems/44390/binsey-poplars

The children taught themselves how to resist – John Berger, foreword to *Faithful Witnesses* (ed. Kamal Boulatta), quoted in Juman Simaan, 'John Berger and Everyday Acts of Sumūd' in *Dark Mountain*, https://dark-mountain.net/john-berger-and-everyday-acts-of-sumud/

It's 13:15 – Dmitri Kolesnikov, quoted in Ben Aris, 'Doomed Sailor's Letter from the Kursk', (translator not noted) *Telegraph* (27 October 2000)

Maersk is investing £1bn – Jillian Ambrose, 'Shipping firm Maersk spends £1bn on "carbon neutral" container ships', *Guardian* online (27 August 2021), https://www.theguardian.com/business/2021/aug/24/worlds-biggest-shipping-firm-maersk-in-1bn-green-push

Resourceful people – Caroline Eden, *Samarkand: Recipes and Stories from Central Asia and the Caucasus* (Kyle Books, 2016)

You might just as well say – Lewis Carroll, *Alice's Adventures in Wonderland* (Wordsworth, 2018)

September
Human beings do not go hand in hand – Virginia Woolf, 'On Being Ill', op. cit.

Ok glacier – see Andri Snaer Magnason, 'Letter to the Future'; data on climate change from Spencer Weart, *The Discovery of Global Warming* (Harvard University Press, 2003)

the common-white willow – John Evelyn, op. cit.

break and snap off – Charlotte Du Cann, *52 Flowers that Shook my World* (Two Ravens, 2012)

no matter how warm – Stephen Rutt, *The Eternal Season* (Elliott and Thompson, 2021) a subdued repetition – Earl Grey, *The Charm of Birds* (Hodder and Stoughton, 1927)

cheared my bed-room – Dorothy Wordsworth, journal for February 1835, in Polly Atkin, *Recovering Dorothy: The Hidden Life of Dorothy Wordsworth* (Saraband, 2021)

Make a small Cross – *Pennsylvania Gazette*, 19 October 1752

the only city in the world – Len Deighton, *Funeral in Berlin* (Jonathan Cape, 1964)

the art of losing – see Elizabeth Bishop, 'One Art', *Complete Poems* (Chatto & Windus, 2011)

shelly mound – Robert Hooke, op. cit.

Friendship is a sheltering tree – Samuel Taylor Coleridge, 'Youth and Age' at Poetry Foundation, https://www.poetryfoundation.org/poems/44000/youth-and-age-56d222ebca145

A curious optical deception – 'The velocity of the apparent motion of the visible portions of the spokes is proportionate to the velocity of the wheel itself; but it varies in different parts of the curve: and might therefore, if accurately estimated, furnish new modes of measuring the duration of the impressions of light on the retina.' – P. M. Roget, *Explanation of an optical deception in the appearance of the spokes of a wheel seen through vertical apertures, Phil. Trans. R. Soc. Lond.* 1825, 1 January 1825, Part V

the general open Knight's tour problem – A knight's tour is a sequence of moves on a chessboard in which the knight visits every square only once. If the knight ends on a square that is one knight's move from the beginning square (so that it could tour the board again immediately, following the same path), the tour is *closed*, otherwise it is *open*

composition for handbells – John Cage, Carillon No. 5 (1967), available on Peters Edition EP 6803

what would I miss – from *Sobbing Superpower: Selected Poems* by Tadeusz Różewicz, translated by Joanna Trzeciak

Act in accordance – Kathan Brown (Cage's printer), *John Cage. Visual Art: To Sober and Quiet the Mind* (Crown Point Press, 2000)

It is easy enough to say – Matsuo Bashō, 'Records of a Travel-Worn Satchel', in *The Narrow Road to the Deep North*, translated by Nobuyuki Yuasa (Penguin, 1966)

ABOUT THE AUTHOR

NANCY CAMPBELL is a poet and non-fiction writer whose books include *Fifty Words for Snow*, a Waterstones Book of the Month, *The Library of Ice: Readings from a Cold Climate*, *Disko Bay* and *How to Say 'I Love You' in Greenlandic*. She was appointed Canal Laureate in 2018, writing poems for installation across the UK waterways from London Docklands to the River Severn, and received the Ness Award from the Royal Geographical Society in 2020. She is currently Visiting Professor of Literature at the Free University, Berlin.

www.nancycampbell.co.uk